REAL WORLD SELLING™

Techniques for Selling in the Real World—*with real results!*

Rick Wilcoxon

Real-World Selling™
Techniques for Selling in the Real World—*with real results!*

Cover graphic sourced from www.Corbis.com
Cover design by EditWriteDesign.com

First Edition

ISBN: 1491266279
ISBN-13: 978-1491266274

Acknowledgements

I owe far more gratitude than I can express to the many clients that have had faith in my concepts and trusted that I could make a difference in the performance of their salespeople. I appreciate you all.

I am especially grateful to my editor, Dehanna Bailee, with EditWriteDesign, for her patience, expert advice, and her many helpful suggestions.

For my daughter, Lissa,
whom, as a teenager, once referred to
me as "a *model* salesperson:
a small replica of the real thing!"

Contents

i

Introduction

Tech #		Tech #	
1	End All Answers	24	Defending Competitors
2	The Purpose for Calling	25	When Clients Complain
3	Not Interested	26	If a Client Even Hints
4	Hint Phrases	27	Customer Benefits
5	More Appointments	28	Claims
6	A Significant Impact	29	Underselling™
7	Initial Contact	30	Define Your
8	Rapport		Differences
9	Benefit Statement with a Hope of Gain	31	Cushions
		32	Q-A-Q
10	Benefit Statement with a Fear of Loss	33	I Am Glad You…
		34	Yes, But and Yes, However
11	Curiosity Opener with a Hope of Gain	35	I Understand How You Feel
12	Curiosity Opener with a Fear of Loss	36	Keep a Record of What You Learn
13	Association/Benefit Statement	37	Referrals
14	Ask Permission	38	Seven-Nevers
15	Open-Ended Questions	39	As Promised
16	Problem-Related Questions	40	Involve the Referring Person
17	One Question at a Time	41	Keep the Referring Person in the Loop
18	Why?		
19	Follow a Closed-Ended Question	42	Confirming Appointments
20	Insurance Question™	43	Negative Emotion Words
21	Situation Questions		
22	Picture Questions™	44	Describing the Price
23	Zero-To-Ten Question™	45	Interests and Specifics

Contents

ii

Tech #

46 Call Someone Who Did Not Buy
47 Rule of Six
48 Ask to be Introduced
49 Testimonial Book
50 A Quick Moment
51 May I Make a Suggestion?
52 Do Something
53 Odd Times
54 Reverse the Introduction
55 A Copy of Your Notes
56 Detail Questions
57 Situation Questions
58 Solution-Related Questions
59 Qualification Summary
60 Referral Letter
61 Buying Signals
62 Trial Closes
63 Does the Client Know that I Know…?
64 Leave No Doubt
65 Stand at a Slight Angle
66 Stand Directly in Front
67 Have a Seat
68 Eye-Contact
69 Entertainment Options
70 The *Real* Objection

Tech #

71 Prospects
72 Practice Responding to Objections
73 Compliments
74 Your Mama Taught You Right
75 Your Mama Really Taught You Right
76 Your Mama Would be Proud of You
77 Hold On to Your Brochure
78 Six Types of Evidence
79 Seven Methods to Capture Attention
80 Work the Chair
81 Introduce Yourself— Really?
82 Confirmation Questions
83 Acknowledgement Questions
84 The Client's Agenda
85 The Client's Time
86 Silence
87 Feel—Felt—Found
88 Smile—Pause—Cushion
89 Be Willing to Leave
90 How Are You Today?
91 Problems?

Contents

iii

Tech #

92 Always a Benefit
93 Service
94 Two or More Weeks from Now
95 Proprietary Information
96 Four Price Options
97 When Forced to Drop the Price
98 Reduction to the Difference
99 Reduction to the Ridiculous
100 The Alternative

Tech #

101 The Comparison
102 Not in the Budget
103 Proud Surprise
104 Reverse
105 We're Happy with…
106 Call Me… (Another Time)
107 Send Information
108 Focus Groups
109 Work Smarter, Not Harder—Really?
110 Enthusiasm
111 Service Letter

Introduction

I am a salesperson. I started my career in 1972 selling memberships to a fraternal organization, door-to-door. Suffice it to say, it was a great training ground for rejection, although I quickly realized how much I enjoyed the challenge of persuasion.

After a year of door-to-door sales, I accepted a position selling equipment to telephone companies. It was then I learned many of my account-development skills, being that there were a limited number of telephone companies in my territory. In order to make more money, I had to learn how to gain more business from my existing customers.

I began my career in the sales training industry in 1980. Since then, I have called on salespeople and management at all levels throughout the world. I have made thousands of joint-sales calls with others to critique their selling skills and, as a result, I have witnessed some very talented professional salespeople. I have also had the chance to critique many unskilled (and even clueless) salespeople, as well.

I have trained over 400,000 salespeople throughout the world and there are probably not many sales techniques I have not seen or heard. I do not know everything about sales. No one does. However, I have learned a lot; and hopefully, this book will help you profit from my experiences.

The techniques outlined in this book are based on the concepts introduced in **The *Real-World Selling*™ Seminar**. Since 1983, these ideas have made a significant impact on the success of thousands of salespeople worldwide who represent hundreds of products and services.

Note that the concepts in this book are not on trial. They have been proven to work for many thousands of people. It is actually *you* who is on trial, and the real question is: Will you do what is necessary to make these concepts work for you?

I recommend you select one idea at a time from this book and then apply the idea repeatedly for a period of two weeks with your clients and potential customers. Through this two-week concentrated effort, you should begin to develop the habit, and thus be able to instill the skill more quickly.

I welcome your feedback and look forward to learning about your successes.

Rick A. Wilcoxon
Rick~Alan & Associates
Office: 281-492-1265
Email: rickw@rickalan.com

Caution
Open at your own risk!

The subsequent pages contain language which can deliberately result in powerful imagery. You are therefore warned that opening this material may trigger an expansion of perception and creativity that could result in a permanent life change.

My experiences with applying this concept:

(See Tech #36)

Date: _____

Company: _____

Client(s) Names: _____

_____

What I learned or was reminded: _____

_____

_____

Date: _____

Company: _____

Client(s) Names: _____

_____

What I learned or was reminded: _____

_____

_____

Date: _____

Company: _____

Client(s) Names: _____

_____

What I learned or was reminded: _____

_____

_____

Real-World Selling™ Technique

End All Answers

End all answers with a question. Remember, the person who asks the question controls the conversation.

When you answer a client's question, or initiate a statement, develop the habit of then asking a question of the client (*any kind of question*—either open- or closed-ended).

This does not mean your question should necessarily encourage your client to say, *"Yes,"* as sometimes, *"No,"* is the best answer. Simply encourage your client's involvement and participation in the conversation.

And, this also does not mean that you should ask a question after every sentence. Just make your point—however long that takes—and then ask a question to get a response from the client.

My experiences with applying this concept:

(See Tech #36)

Date: _____

Company: _____

Client(s) Names: _____

_____

What I learned or was reminded: _____

_____

_____

Date: _____

Company: _____

Client(s) Names: _____

_____

What I learned or was reminded: _____

_____

_____

Date: _____

Company: _____

Client(s) Names: _____

_____

What I learned or was reminded: _____

_____

_____

Real-World Selling™ Technique

The Purpose for Calling

The first question on the mind of everyone when receiving a call from a salesperson is, *"Why are you calling me?"*

Think about it.... Have you ever had an existing client ask, *"What's on your mind?"* or *"So, what do you have for me today?"*

What your client was really asking you was *"Why are you calling me?"* or, if you are meeting the client in person, *"Why are you here?"*

Whether speaking to the client in person, or over the phone, establish your agenda for the conversation quickly by telling the client the reason for your call.

State the benefit to the client, and remember this statement is not about your product, service, or your company. It is about what the client might want and how you can be of benefit to them.

Keep the statement general in nature and about something you suspect might be of value to the client.

My experiences with applying this concept:
(See Tech #36)

Date: _____

Company: _____

Client(s) Names: _____

_____

What I learned or was reminded: _____

_____

_____

Date: _____

Company: _____

Client(s) Names: _____

_____

What I learned or was reminded: _____

_____

_____

Date: _____

Company: _____

Client(s) Names: _____

_____

What I learned or was reminded: _____

_____

_____

Real-World Selling™ Technique

Not Interested

The word "interested" tends to shut down the conversation as many clients interpret the word as meaning "commitment."

Realize that when a client is asked if they would be "interested," they may not know enough to make a commitment, so the natural reaction may be, *"I don't know. Why don't you send me something?"* or *"Maybe. Tell me more about it."*

Instead of saying, *"Would you be interested?"* say, *"Would it be something worth discussing?"* This way the client who may not be "interested" may be willing to "discuss" it. They may even be willing to "look into" it, "consider" it, or even "hear" about it.

(Actually, quite often when the client is not interested, it is because the salesperson didn't say anything the client thought was interesting!)

My experiences with applying this concept:
(See Tech #36)

Date: _____

Company: _____

Client(s) Names: _____

_____

What I learned or was reminded: _____

_____

_____

Date: _____

Company: _____

Client(s) Names: _____

_____

What I learned or was reminded: _____

_____

_____

Date: _____

Company: _____

Client(s) Names: _____

_____

What I learned or was reminded: _____

_____

_____

Real-World Selling™ Technique

Hint Phrases

"I would like to…"
"I want(ed) to…"
I need(ed) to…"

These kinds of phrases are all about **you.** What **you** would like, what **you** want, and what **you** need!

Remember…the client may not know anything about you, so why would they care about what **you** would like, what **you** want, or what **you** need?

Instead of hinting about what you would like to do first and then asking a question, simply ask instead.

Example:

"I'd like to meet with you next week (Hint), *would that be all right? (Question)"*

Simply ask, *"Could we meet next week?"*

Do not hint first—go straight to the question!

The hint often gives the client too much time to prepare the answer of, *"No."*

My experiences with applying this concept:
(See Tech #36)

Date: _____

Company: _____

Client(s) Names: _____

_____

What I learned or was reminded: _____

_____

_____

Date: _____

Company: _____

Client(s) Names: _____

_____

What I learned or was reminded: _____

_____

_____

Date: _____

Company: _____

Client(s) Names: _____

_____

What I learned or was reminded: _____

_____

_____

Real-World Selling™ Technique

More Appointments

Avoid the word appointment! This word is much like the word "interested" and often the client tends to assume it means "commitment." (As in, they may be willing to meet with you, but hesitant to commit to an "appointment.")

Using alternative phrasing allows your client to be open to having a discussion about how their company can reduce travel expenses by five percent, without having to commit to an "appointment."

My experiences with applying this concept:

(See Tech #36)

Date: _____

Company: _____

Client(s) Names: _____

_____

What I learned or was reminded: _____

_____

_____

Date: _____

Company: _____

Client(s) Names: _____

_____

What I learned or was reminded: _____

_____

_____

Date: _____

Company: _____

Client(s) Names: _____

_____

What I learned or was reminded: _____

_____

_____

Real-World Selling™ Techni

A Significant Impact

"Impact" implies significance. It implies something dramatic, dynamic, or powerful. "Impact" is one of the most powerful, positive-emotion words that a salesperson can use.

When speaking with a client or potential customer, interject the word "impact" as often as is practical.

Instead of telling them how your company *helps* its clients, explain how your company has an *impact* on their clients' profits or how your products and services can have an *impact* on a company's ability to meet its deadline!

Using the word "impact" provides the client with something to remember and can make a difference in the client's perception of your message.

My experiences with applying this concept:
(See Tech #36)

Date: _____

Company: _____

Client(s) Names: _____

_____

What I learned or was reminded: _____

_____

_____

Date: _____

Company: _____

Client(s) Names: _____

_____

What I learned or was reminded: _____

_____

_____

Date: _____

Company: _____

Client(s) Names: _____

_____

What I learned or was reminded: _____

_____

_____

Real-World Selling™ Technique

Initial Contact

The five steps of Initial Contact are:

1 **Pleasantries**
   Develop rapport and keep it brief. (See Tech #8)

2 **Question**: "At this point...
   a. *What do you know about us?"* or
   b. *How much do you know about us?"* or
   c. *How familiar are you with us?"*
   Make it an Open-Ended Question to learn about the client's perception of your company before telling them anything about you.

   Bridge to Introductory Statement
   "Let me give you a brief overview about us, so you'll know why I'll ask some of the questions I'll be asking, all right?"

3 **Introductory Statement** (30-60 seconds)
   a What you do   d How you do it
   b Your territory   e How you are different
   c Your customers
   State facts and features only and avoid the words "you" and "your." Use "I," "we," and "our." This is all about you, not the client.

4 **Association/Benefit Statement**
   Avoid making promises. (See Tech #13)

5 **Ask Permission To Ask Questions**
   Here's a good chance to use the word "impact."
   (See Tech #6)

My experiences with applying this concept:
(See Tech #36)

Date: _____

Company: _____

Client(s) Names: _____

_____

What I learned or was reminded: _____

_____

_____

Date: _____

Company: _____

Client(s) Names: _____

_____

What I learned or was reminded: _____

_____

_____

Date: _____

Company: _____

Client(s) Names: _____

_____

What I learned or was reminded: _____

_____

_____

Real-World Selling™ Technique

Rapport

Rapport is the process of breaking down barriers and then building common ground. Most salespeople acknowledge that establishing a good rapport with a client is critical, although it is rare that the salesperson has been told exactly *how* to do it.

Whether it takes a period of two minutes or two years, verbal rapport can be more easily accomplished using the following three steps:

1 Encourage the client to talk about themselves (most people know this).

2 Establish or point out the similarities between you and your client, or your company and the client's company (most people do not know this).

3 Ask Open–Ended Questions to encourage your client to talk about the similarities that you have in common with each other.

My experiences with applying this concept:

(See Tech #36)

Date: _____

Company: _____

Client(s) Names: _____

_____

What I learned or was reminded: _____

_____

_____

Date: _____

Company: _____

Client(s) Names: _____

_____

What I learned or was reminded: _____

_____

_____

Date: _____

Company: _____

Client(s) Names: _____

_____

What I learned or was reminded: _____

_____

_____

Real-World Selling™ Techni(

Benefit Statement with a Hope of Gain

In general, people buy for one of two basic reasons: They want to gain something or they hope to avoid losing something. (See Tech [#]10)

State your purpose for calling as a benefit (gain) to the client. (This idea is an illustration of Tech [#]2)

For example:

a. *"We **may** be able to help your company improve the level of service that you provide to your customers."*

b. *"It is **possible** that we can assure you of enough retirement income to continue with your lifestyle."*

Remember, the statement has nothing to do with your product, service, or company. Instead of saying you *"can"* or *"will,"* state that you *"may,"* you *"might,"* or that *"it's possible,"* etc.

And while sometimes salespeople say, *"But I **can** do it!"* realize it is not about whether you can or not. It is more of a matter of whether the client *believes* you can—especially during those early moments of your sales call.

My experiences with applying this concept:

(See Tech #36)

Date: _____

Company: _____

Client(s) Names: _____

_____

What I learned or was reminded: _____

_____

_____

Date: _____

Company: _____

Client(s) Names: _____

_____

What I learned or was reminded: _____

_____

_____

Date: _____

Company: _____

Client(s) Names: _____

_____

What I learned or was reminded: _____

_____

_____

Real-World Selling™ Techniq

Benefit Statement with a Fear of Loss

In general, people buy for one of two basic reasons: They want to gain something (see Tech #9), or they hope to avoid losing something.

State your purpose for calling as a possible loss to the client. (This idea is an illustration of Tech #2)

For example:

*"We **may** be able to minimize the possibility of your company **losing** customers to your larger competitors."*

Realize this statement has nothing to do with your product, service, or company.

(The intent when stating a "Fear of Loss" is not to be a fear monger, but rather to pique the client's curiosity about something with which they may already be concerned.)

My experiences with applying this concept:
(See Tech #36) ⟹

Date: _____

Company: _____

Client(s) Names: _____

_____

What I learned or was reminded: _____

_____

_____

Date: _____

Company: _____

Client(s) Names: _____

_____

What I learned or was reminded: _____

_____

_____

Date: _____

Company: _____

Client(s) Names: _____

_____

What I learned or was reminded: _____

_____

_____

Real-World Selling™ Techniq

Curiosity Opener with a Hope of Gain

A Curiosity Opener is similar to a Benefit Statement in that it is a **statement** that is designed to arouse the client's curiosity, but without actually stating the benefit to the client.

For example:

a. *"I have an idea that I'm certain you're going to like."*

b. *"I think you'll be excited about what our company is about to introduce."*

c. *"I thought you might like to know there are a few major changes about to be implemented that could be profitable for you."*

d. *"You will not believe what I heard yesterday."*

   (Only make this comment, if you believe that your client will not perceive it as gossip.)

e. *"I heard a very positive compliment about you."*

My experiences with applying this concept:
(See Tech #36)

Date: _____

Company: _____

Client(s) Names: _____

_____

What I learned or was reminded: _____

_____

_____

Date: _____

Company: _____

Client(s) Names: _____

_____

What I learned or was reminded: _____

_____

_____

Date: _____

Company: _____

Client(s) Names: _____

_____

What I learned or was reminded: _____

_____

_____

Real-World Selling™ Technique

Curiosity Opener with a Fear of Loss

A "Fear of Loss" Curiosity Opener is much like other Curiosity Openers, but implies a possible concern to the client. It is yet another method to arouse the client's curiosity and focus their attention.

For example:

a. *"I have an idea to discuss with you that I thought you'd like to hear before your competitors learn about it."*

b. *"We have heard about a few changes that are going to take place in the market that may affect the way you do business."*

(As with the Benefit Statement, the intent when stating a "Fear of Loss" is not to be a fear monger, but rather to pique the client's curiosity about something with which they may be already concerned.)

My experiences with applying this concept:

(See Tech #36)

Date: _____

Company: _____

Client(s) Names: _____

_____

What I learned or was reminded: _____

_____

_____

Date: _____

Company: _____

Client(s) Names: _____

_____

What I learned or was reminded: _____

_____

_____

Date: _____

Company: _____

Client(s) Names: _____

_____

What I learned or was reminded: _____

_____

_____

Real-World Selling™ Technic

Association/Benefit Statement

Before stating a benefit to the client, whether it is voiced as a "Hope of Gain" or as a "Fear of Loss," you might provide a context prior to the benefit. (This idea is an example of Tips #2 & #9)

It is the Association (context) that tends to make the Benefit Statement more conversational and allows the client to better relate to your benefit.

For example:

"Most managers say they're always looking for ways to improve the service they offer their customers (Association). *We **may** be able to help your company improve on the level of service that you're able to provide* (Benefit)."

Typically, the client will tend to accept the context, which then makes it more likely that they will be more open to what you would like to discuss.

My experiences with applying this concept:

(See Tech #36)

Date: _____

Company: _____

Client(s) Names: _____

_____

What I learned or was reminded: _____

_____

_____

Date: _____

Company: _____

Client(s) Names: _____

_____

What I learned or was reminded: _____

_____

_____

Date: _____

Company: _____

Client(s) Names: _____

_____

What I learned or was reminded: _____

_____

_____

Real-World Selling™ Techniqu

Ask Permission

Before asking a series of questions, ask permission first. Do not be concerned that the client may say, *"No,"* for if you first provide an appropriate reason for the client to talk to you, the chance of them saying, *"No,"* is very unlikely.

Asking the client for permission to ask questions also accomplishes numerous objectives:

1. The client will tend to relax because they will have a better understanding of the process you will take.

2. You will define the agenda of the conversation.

3. You will pique the client's curiosity about what you may ask.

4. You will be in control of the conversation.

Example of asking permission:

"So that we can better determine just how much of an impact we can have on your project deadline, may I get your answers to a few questions?"

My experiences with applying this concept:
(See Tech #36)

Date: _____

Company: _____

Client(s) Names: _____

_____

What I learned or was reminded: _____

_____

_____

Date: _____

Company: _____

Client(s) Names: _____

_____

What I learned or was reminded: _____

_____

_____

Date: _____

Company: _____

Client(s) Names: _____

_____

What I learned or was reminded: _____

_____

_____

Real-World Selling™ Techniqu

Open-Ended Questions

Open-Ended Questions send the message that you are interested in the client and in their situation.

Approximately eighty percent of your questions should be Open-Ended, as they encourage more client involvement and allow the salesperson the opportunity to gather even more information.

They also can help you avoid the impression that you are "leading" the client with your inquiry.

Examples of Open-Ended Questions:

Who	Tell me about…	For instance?
What	Explain…	Such as?
When	Describe…	And?
Where	Elaborate…	Oh?
Why	Help me…	Which…
How	For example?	

My experiences with applying this concept:
(See Tech #36)

Date: _____

Company: _____

Client(s) Names: _____

_____

What I learned or was reminded: _____

_____

_____

Date: _____

Company: _____

Client(s) Names: _____

_____

What I learned or was reminded: _____

_____

_____

Date: _____

Company: _____

Client(s) Names: _____

_____

What I learned or was reminded: _____

_____

_____

Real-World Selling™ Techniqu

Problem-Related Questions

Problem-Related Questions are questions that encourage a client to elaborate *further* about their point of dissatisfaction.

Examples of Problem-Related Questions:

a *"Why do/did you say that?"*

b *"Can you tell me more about that?"*

c *"What other problems does/did that create?"*

d *"Who else does/did that affect?"*

e *"How much of a problem is/was that?"*

f *"What is/was your management's reaction to that?"*

g *"How long have you had to deal with that?"*

h *"What happened after that?"*

i *"Why do you suppose that happened?"*

The use of Problem-Related Questions will help the client realize that you want to know more about their situation.

Do not be too eager to jump into your presentation phase. Be sure to ask two to four consecutive Problem-Related Questions each time the client voices a point of dissatisfaction. Learn more about the client's situation first—you can always present your product or service later.

My experiences with applying this concept:

(See Tech #36)

Date: _____

Company: _____

Client(s) Names: _____

_____

What I learned or was reminded: _____

_____

_____

Date: _____

Company: _____

Client(s) Names: _____

_____

What I learned or was reminded: _____

_____

_____

Date: _____

Company: _____

Client(s) Names: _____

_____

What I learned or was reminded: _____

_____

_____

Real-World Selling™ Technique

One Question at a Time

It is a natural tendency to ask a question and "expect" a particular answer. Consequently, this means one tends to structure their questions to *help* the client with the answer one "expects" or "wants" to hear.

General Rule: Ask one question at a time and then wait for the client to answer.

An example of the wrong way:

"How many vendors are you presently working with? Is it just one, or are there more than that?"

An example of the right way:

"How many vendors are you presently working with?"

Do not fill in the blanks for the client, as it typically "closes-off" the question and does not serve your purpose of gathering information. It is also not very professional and some may be annoyed by it.

(This is a common mistake salespeople make. The longer the question, the more likely it will be Closed-Ended. Keep your questions short and, if at all possible, Open-Ended.)

My experiences with applying this concept:
(See Tech #36)

Date: _____

Company: _____

Client(s) Names: _____

_____

What I learned or was reminded: _____

_____

_____

Date: _____

Company: _____

Client(s) Names: _____

_____

What I learned or was reminded: _____

_____

_____

Date: _____

Company: _____

Client(s) Names: _____

_____

What I learned or was reminded: _____

_____

_____

Real-World Selling™ Technique

Why?

Have you ever asked someone, *"Why did you do that?"* only to have them respond, *"Look, I did the best I could!"*

The question "Why?" tends to refocus your conversation away from the subject and onto the person. It also tends to encourage the client to become defensive and justify their answer because the conversation suddenly focused on *them*.

The question "Why?" can be a powerful question though, if the client's answer serves your purpose

For example:

> *"Why are you unhappy with your current vendor?"*

That question will tend to encourage the client to *justify* their dissatisfaction about your competitor.

General Rule: Only ask the question, "Why?" if the answer will work to your advantage. Never ask it if the answer works against you.

So, before asking "Why?" first determine: *"Will the answer serve my purpose?"* Be assured, you will know the answer to that question before you ask.

My experiences with applying this concept:
(See Tech #36)

Date: _____

Company: _____

Client(s) Names: _____

_____

What I learned or was reminded: _____

_____

_____

Date: _____

Company: _____

Client(s) Names: _____

_____

What I learned or was reminded: _____

_____

_____

Date: _____

Company: _____

Client(s) Names: _____

_____

What I learned or was reminded: _____

_____

_____

Real-World Selling™ Technique

Follow a Closed-Ended Question

There is nothing necessarily wrong with a Closed-Ended Question. It is just that salespeople tend to ask too many of them—and they often ask them for the wrong reasons.

Closed-Ended Questions are best used to *guide* or *direct* the conversation. So, after the client answers your Closed-Ended Question, follow it up with an Open-Ended Question to encourage more involvement and interaction from your client.

Guide the conversation in the direction you want, and then ask the client an Open-Ended Question to learn more about the client's opinion or their reaction.

For example:

You: *"Does this approach make sense?"* (Closed-Ended Question)

Client: *"Yeah, I would say so."*

You: *"Good. What is it that you like the most about it?"* (Open-Ended Question)

My experiences with applying this concept:
(See Tech #36)

Date: _____

Company: _____

Client(s) Names: _____

_____

What I learned or was reminded: _____

_____

_____

Date: _____

Company: _____

Client(s) Names: _____

_____

What I learned or was reminded: _____

_____

_____

Date: _____

Company: _____

Client(s) Names: _____

_____

What I learned or was reminded: _____

_____

_____

Real-World Selling™ Technique

Insurance Question™

Ask this question *before* starting any conversation regarding price to position your company as being similar to the client's company. This kind of question is called an "Insurance Question™" because, like insurance, it is established before it is needed.

The Insurance Question™:

You: *"Who do you compete with?"*
Client: *"Companies ABC and DEF."*
You: *"Are you always the cheapest?"*
Client: *"No, usually not. Most of the time we're about 15% more than our competition."*
You: *"Why do you think your customers choose you instead of doing business with them?"*

The client will then typically justify the same reasons why you are not the cheapest in your business and later, if your client questions your price, you can point out how your ways of doing business are similar to the way the client does business.

(It is just not reasonable for someone to expect their own customers to pay more for quality, service, or experience, but then expect you to charge less for the same thing.)

My experiences with applying this concept:

(See Tech #36)

Date: _____

Company: _____

Client(s) Names: _____

_____

What I learned or was reminded: _____

_____

_____

Date: _____

Company: _____

Client(s) Names: _____

_____

What I learned or was reminded: _____

_____

_____

Date: _____

Company: _____

Client(s) Names: _____

_____

What I learned or was reminded: _____

_____

_____

Real-World Selling™ Technique

Situation Questions

Often, the client or potential client will not volunteer their point of dissatisfaction (P.O.D.). This is why it is essential to ask Situation Questions to learn of any possible P.O.D. A Situation Question is: Any question *designed* to uncover or identify a client's point of dissatisfaction.

For example:

a *"How pleased are you with the level of service you receive from your current vendors?"*

b *"When you have backorders, what complications does that create for you?"*

c *"How often do you not receive the quality you expected?"*

d *"If you could eliminate one difficulty from your last project, what would it be?"*

Realize that just because you ask a Situation Question, it does not mean the client will have a point of dissatisfaction—but, how will you know unless you ask?

(Avoid asking Closed-Ended Situation Questions! They make it easy for the client to avoid admitting any dissatisfaction.)

My experiences with applying this concept:
(See Tech #36)

Date: _____

Company: _____

Client(s) Names: _____

_____

What I learned or was reminded: _____

_____

_____

Date: _____

Company: _____

Client(s) Names: _____

_____

What I learned or was reminded: _____

_____

_____

Date: _____

Company: _____

Client(s) Names: _____

_____

What I learned or was reminded: _____

_____

_____

Real-World Selling™ Techniqu

Picture Questions™

A Picture Question™ is a powerful question because it *requires* the client to imagine the benefit of your idea before they can answer the question.

The structure of the Picture Question™ is as follows:

1 *"Let us suppose..."* or *"What if..."* or *"If..."*
2 Mention solving the client's point of dissatisfaction.
3 Ask *"How..."* or *"What..."*

For example:

"What if you received all your materials at the time you needed them? How would that affect your project deadlines?"

(Remember, a Picture Question™ should be Open-Ended, because a Closed-Ended Picture Question™ can be interpreted as very leading and condescending, plus the client often will not imagine the benefit.)

An example of a Closed-Ended Picture Question™:

"What if you received all your materials at the time you needed them? Do you think that would be better?"

(I don't know about you, but that Closed-Ended Question seems awfully condescending.)

My experiences with applying this concept:
(See Tech #36) ⟹

Date: _____

Company: _____

Client(s) Names: _____

_____

What I learned or was reminded: _____

_____

_____

Date: _____

Company: _____

Client(s) Names: _____

_____

What I learned or was reminded: _____

_____

_____

Date: _____

Company: _____

Client(s) Names: _____

_____

What I learned or was reminded: _____

_____

_____

Real-World Selling™ Technique

Zero-To-Ten Question™

A Zero-To-Ten Question™ is an excellent method to learn about a client's point(s) of dissatisfaction (P.O.D.). Whenever someone rates anything, it automatically calls attention to what the "thing" is *not*.

The Zero-To-Ten Question™ is a two-part question.

For example:

1   *"How would you rate __(possible P.O.D.)__ (the quality, service, reliability, maintenance, ease of use, etc.) on a scale of zero to ten, with ten being perfect; and, of course, nothing is perfect?"*

   Client chooses a number. *(Typically "7" or "8.")*

2   *"Why not higher?"*

Notes:

1   Do not ask this question too early in the sales call. The earlier you ask, the higher the number a client will tend to choose.

2   Be prepared to have the client rate numerous possible P.O.D.S; and the number "10" *must* be defined as *"perfect."*

My experiences with applying this concept:
(See Tech #36)

Date: _____

Company: _____

Client(s) Names: _____

_____

What I learned or was reminded: _____

_____

_____

Date: _____

Company: _____

Client(s) Names: _____

_____

What I learned or was reminded: _____

_____

_____

Date: _____

Company: _____

Client(s) Names: _____

_____

What I learned or was reminded: _____

_____

_____

Real-World Selling™ Technique

Defending Competitors

Salespeople are typically optimistic people with positive attitudes; and when a client or prospective client voices a negative comment about a competitor, they often tend to respond with a positive comment about the competitor to "balance" the client's statement. For example:

Client: *"With the recent changes in the market, it seems that XYZ is only concerned about us when we're spending a lot of money with them."*

Salesperson: *"Well, that's too bad, because they usually treat their customers better than that."*

In other words, you just told the client, *"You should give them another chance, because I know my competitor and they are better than that!"* Is that really the message you want to give to your client?

It is **not** your job to defend your competitor. And, it is also not your job to say anything negative about them either.

Instead, show empathy with your client's situation, as doing so may encourage your client to continue to complain so you can gain more information about the client's point(s) of dissatisfaction.

My experiences with applying this concept:
(See Tech #36) ➤

Date: _____

Company: _____

Client(s) Names: _____

_____

What I learned or was reminded: _____

_____

_____

Date: _____

Company: _____

Client(s) Names: _____

_____

What I learned or was reminded: _____

_____

_____

Date: _____

Company: _____

Client(s) Names: _____

_____

What I learned or was reminded: _____

_____

_____

Real-World Selling™ Technique

When Clients Complain

If a client complains about a competitor (yours or theirs), act shocked or concerned. Once you act shocked or concerned, the message the client receives is that you *never* hear that, you are surprised, or, at the least, disappointed to learn about it.

Not doing so will make it appear to the client that you are used to hearing that comment and you may become aligned with the complaint. The client could then assume they will have the same complaint with you.

Another benefit of acting shocked or concerned is that the client may tend to complain more about your competitor because they will assume you are interested in hearing about it (and, hopefully, you are).

Also, when you act shocked or concerned, a client may even elaborate more about their point of dissatisfaction in an attempt to convince you, because they may assume you doubt what they are saying to you.

My experiences with applying this concept:
(See Tech #36)

Date: _____

Company: _____

Client(s) Names: _____

_____

What I learned or was reminded: _____

_____

_____

Date: _____

Company: _____

Client(s) Names: _____

_____

What I learned or was reminded: _____

_____

_____

Date: _____

Company: _____

Client(s) Names: _____

_____

What I learned or was reminded: _____

_____

_____

Real-World Selling™ Technique

If a Client Even Hints

Salespeople are often too anxious to introduce their product or service and jump at any opportunity to help the client.

When a client voices a point of dissatisfaction, avoid trying to immediately "fix" it with your product or service. Instead, encourage the client to tell you more about their situation.

Let the client know you are focused on learning about their business, instead of simply selling them your product or service at the earliest opportunity.

Listen to your client's complaints first and stay out of your presentation phase for as long as possible. You can always present your product or service later in the conversation.

My experiences with applying this concept:
(See Tech #36)

Date: _____

Company: _____

Client(s) Names: _____

_____

What I learned or was reminded: _____

_____

_____

Date: _____

Company: _____

Client(s) Names: _____

_____

What I learned or was reminded: _____

_____

_____

Date: _____

Company: _____

Client(s) Names: _____

_____

What I learned or was reminded: _____

_____

_____

Real-World Selling™ Techniq

Customer Benefits

Stating a benefit to the customer is the most basic concept in sales. When presented with a new or different idea, the natural question on a client's mind is often, *"Why should I care about that?"*

Even as you read this book, you have likely asked yourself, *"What is the benefit to me if I use that technique?"* or *"How will it help me?"*

A Customer Benefit starts with the words:

"You," "Your," "You are," or "You will...."

General Rule: After telling anyone anything, always tell them why they should care.

For example:

"I will fax this to you in five minutes (Fact), *so you will have the information for your meeting this afternoon* (Customer Benefit—why they will care). *"*

This concept is fundamental and rooted in our upbringing. You have probably heard a parent say to a child, *"Eat all your vegetables, so you can grow up to be big and strong"* (which is why the child cares).

Or, *"Go get your shoes on, so you can go outside"* (which, again, is why the child cares).

My experiences with applying this concept:

(See Tech #36)

Date: _____

Company: _____

Client(s) Names: _____

_____

What I learned or was reminded: _____

_____

_____

Date: _____

Company: _____

Client(s) Names: _____

_____

What I learned or was reminded: _____

_____

_____

Date: _____

Company: _____

Client(s) Names: _____

_____

What I learned or was reminded: _____

_____

_____

Real-World Selling™ Techniqu

Claims

Claims are opinions, and are subjective. Do not expect someone to buy from you because it is your *opinion* they should. There is a time to voice a claim—just not during your presentation phase.

Whether the claim is true or not is not the point—what is important is what the client *believes*.

State the specific facts or features when presenting your ideas, and avoid the use of claims (opinions).

For example:

Instead of saying to a client: *"We're the largest company in our industry* (Which may be true, but it is still a claim.)."

Say: *"We have twenty-five offices throughout the country, with over ten-million dollars in total inventory* (Fact). *So, you will be less likely to receive a backorder when you need your materials quickly* (Customer Benefit). "

You may have noticed that the Customer Benefit is actually a claim. This is acceptable because a specific Fact was stated first, which then makes the claim more believable.

My experiences with applying this concept:

(See Tech #36)

Date: _____

Company: _____

Client(s) Names: _____

_____

What I learned or was reminded: _____

_____

_____

Date: _____

Company: _____

Client(s) Names: _____

_____

What I learned or was reminded: _____

_____

_____

Date: _____

Company: _____

Client(s) Names: _____

_____

What I learned or was reminded: _____

_____

_____

Real-World Selling™ Techniqu

Underselling™

The Principle of Underselling™ is: "First state what your product, service, or idea is not. Then tell what it is and be very specific."

When a salesperson states something that they are *not*, they automatically tend to have more credibility when they then say what they *are*.

Underselling™ is the most credible technique available to salespeople when presenting an idea and, consequently, is the reason this technique is frequently used in television, radio, and print advertising.

For example:

> *"We do not have an office nearby, but we do have twenty-five offices throughout the country, with over ten million dollars in total inventory* (Underselling™/Fact). *So, you will be less likely to receive a backorder when you need your materials quickly* (Customer Benefit)."

General Rule: Avoid Underselling™ in response to a client's negative comment or negative question.

Doing so may give the client the impression that you are contradicting them, and it may be perceived that you are saying, *"Yes, but…"* (See Tech #34)

My experiences with applying this concept:

(See Tech #36) ➡

Date: _____

Company: _____

Client(s) Names: _____

_____

What I learned or was reminded: _____

_____

_____

Date: _____

Company: _____

Client(s) Names: _____

_____

What I learned or was reminded: _____

_____

_____

Date: _____

Company: _____

Client(s) Names: _____

_____

What I learned or was reminded: _____

_____

_____

Real-World Selling™ Technique

Define Your Differences

When meeting a prospective client, a common statement that salespeople hear is: *"So, tell me about your company."*

Realize that the client has actually asked two questions:

1 *"Who are you?"*
2 *"How are you different from your competition?"*

If you do not explain how you are different, the client will try to learn it from your competitors.

General Rule: You will have the opportunity to pursue a client's business because of your similarities, but you will be awarded their business because of your differences.

Most salespeople talk about their differences. What they do not do is promote their differences as *the reason* the client should do business with them.

Focus on how you are *different*—not only on who you are and what you do.

My experiences with applying this concept:
(See Tech #36)

Date: _____

Company: _____

Client(s) Names: _____

_____

What I learned or was reminded: _____

_____

_____

Date: _____

Company: _____

Client(s) Names: _____

_____

What I learned or was reminded: _____

_____

_____

Date: _____

Company: _____

Client(s) Names: _____

_____

What I learned or was reminded: _____

_____

_____

Real-World Selling™ Technique

Cushions

Respond to a negative comment or question with a "Cushion," which is: *Something that is said or done to show respect for the negative and begin to drop the client's (and your) defenses.* (A Cushion should be a statement, not a question.)

It is natural that when a person expects an argument, they tend to become more defensive. Avoid the trap of defending a negative comment or question. Show respect for the negative, and then encouraging the person to discuss it.

For example:

Client: *"I am happy with my current supplier. Why should I do business with you?"*

You: *"I really didn't intend to disrupt the relationship you already have (Cushion). Can you tell me what it is you look for in a vendor?"*

My experiences with applying this concept:
(See Tech #36)

Date: _____

Company: _____

Client(s) Names: _____

_____

What I learned or was reminded: _____

_____

_____

Date: _____

Company: _____

Client(s) Names: _____

_____

What I learned or was reminded: _____

_____

_____

Date: _____

Company: _____

Client(s) Names: _____

_____

What I learned or was reminded: _____

_____

_____

Real-World Selling™ Techniq

Q-A-Q

When a client asks a question, first show respect for it by responding with a Cushion (Tech #31). Then apply the Q-A-Q process below to stay in control of the conversation.

The Process:

Q (Question)   **A** (Answer)   **Q** (Question)

Example:

Client: *"Your prices are too high."*

You: *"Well, let's talk about that* (Cushion). *Can you tell me how much more our price is?* (Question)"

Client: *"Yeah. You're about fifteen percent more."*

You: *"Thank you for telling me* (Another Cushion). *Actually, when you consider that the maintenance costs of our system is only sixty percent of that of our competition, in the long run we're actually ten to fifteen percent less than anyone else* (Answer). *So you'll end up saving money each year, compared to what you're spending now.* (Customer Benefit)"

You: *"Can I explain how we accomplish that?* (Question)"

My experiences with applying this concept:
(See Tech #36)

Date: _____

Company: _____

Client(s) Names: _____

_____

What I learned or was reminded: _____

_____

_____

Date: _____

Company: _____

Client(s) Names: _____

_____

What I learned or was reminded: _____

_____

_____

Date: _____

Company: _____

Client(s) Names: _____

_____

What I learned or was reminded: _____

_____

_____

Real-World Selling™ Techniq

I Am Glad You...
(...asked that, said that, told me that, etc.)

"I am glad you...." is a phrase that has been overused and abused by salespeople. And because it is doubtful the client actually *believes* you are glad, the client may also perceive your comment as condescending.

Instead, try voicing a different Cushion, such as:

a *"I understand your concern."*
b *"You have raised a valid point."*
c *"That depends on several factors."*
d *"Well, let us talk about that."*
e *"That is a tough question."*
f *"Not many people think to ask that."*

(Understand that these are just examples and will not apply to every negative comment; they might even be inappropriate at times.)

My experiences with applying this concept:

(See Tech #36) ⟹

Date: _____

Company: _____

Client(s) Names: _____

_____

What I learned or was reminded: _____

_____

_____

Date: _____

Company: _____

Client(s) Names: _____

_____

What I learned or was reminded: _____

_____

_____

Date: _____

Company: _____

Client(s) Names: _____

_____

What I learned or was reminded: _____

_____

_____

Real-World Selling™ Technique

Yes, But and Yes, However

When either of these two phrases is said, the client will most likely interpret the comment to mean one of three things:

a *I don't care.*

b *I'm not listening.*

c *You're wrong.*

Which one of those interpretations do you think will endear you to your client? Right! None of them!

No one likes to be told they are wrong and, while that may not be your intention, when you say, *"Yes, but..."* or *"Yes, however..."* that is exactly what the client might think you said.

Don't let these phrases negate what the client has said. Use a different Cushion for a better result. (See Tech #31)

My experiences with applying this concept:
(See Tech #36) ➡

Date: _____

Company: _____

Client(s) Names: _____

_____

What I learned or was reminded: _____

_____

_____

Date: _____

Company: _____

Client(s) Names: _____

_____

What I learned or was reminded: _____

_____

_____

Date: _____

Company: _____

Client(s) Names: _____

_____

What I learned or was reminded: _____

_____

_____

Real-World Selling™ Technique

I Understand How You Feel

When you say to someone, *"I understand how you feel,"* it tends to minimize the other person's feelings.

The main problem with this phrase are the words *"how you feel."* There's nothing terribly wrong with saying, *"I understand,"* although you probably do not; still, no one wants their feelings to be minimized.

And, although a person usually means well when saying it, the other person may likely think, *"You have no idea how I feel..."* or, at the very least, will not appreciate hearing it.

Examples of other phrases to use:

   a *"I understand your concern."*

   b *"I understand that's not what you were hoping."*

   c *"I understand that's more than you were expecting."*

My experiences with applying this concept:
(See Tech #36) ➡

Date: _____

Company: _____

Client(s) Names: _____

_____

What I learned or was reminded: _____

_____

_____

Date: _____

Company: _____

Client(s) Names: _____

_____

What I learned or was reminded: _____

_____

_____

Date: _____

Company: _____

Client(s) Names: _____

_____

What I learned or was reminded: _____

_____

_____

Real-World Selling™ Technique

Keep a Record of What You Learn

Even if you do not make the sale, you should try to learn something from every sales call. Keep a journal or a record of the following information after each sales call:

1 Date

2 Name of the company

3 Name of the person(s) I met with

4 One or more lessons I learned as a result of this call; or something I already knew that was reinforced

By recording these kinds of details, your experience will be more easily remembered, plus you will tend to reduce the chances that of having to "learn" the same lesson twice.

(You may even be able to build a good foundation to write your own book on sales tips!)

My experiences with applying this concept:
(See Tech #36)

Date: _____

Company: _____

Client(s) Names: _____

_____

What I learned or was reminded: _____

_____

_____

Date: _____

Company: _____

Client(s) Names: _____

_____

What I learned or was reminded: _____

_____

_____

Date: _____

Company: _____

Client(s) Names: _____

_____

What I learned or was reminded: _____

_____

_____

Real-World Selling™ Technique

Referrals

Salespeople are often hesitant to ask for referrals. They seem to think that asking might jeopardize a relationship, or maybe that asking will make them appear desperate. Regardless of the reason of why *not* to ask, ask for referrals anyway.

As long as you ask in a respectful manner, that will not make the client uncomfortable, asking for a referral rarely turns out to have a negative effect.

How to ask for a referral:

"Whom do you know who might at least like to know (hear) about… (what we do, our services, our system, our programs, the kind of quality we provide, etc.)"

Once you have asked this question, then shut up!

The longer the silence, the better the chance you will receive one or more name (referral). The reason the person is silent is because they are trying to think of someone to refer to you. (It makes no sense to stop them from thinking!)

My experiences with applying this concept:

(See Tech #36)

Date: _____

Company: _____

Client(s) Names: _____

_____

What I learned or was reminded: _____

_____

_____

Date: _____

Company: _____

Client(s) Names: _____

_____

What I learned or was reminded: _____

_____

_____

Date: _____

Company: _____

Client(s) Names: _____

_____

What I learned or was reminded: _____

_____

_____

Real-World Selling™ Technique

Seven-Nevers

There are seven words and/or phrases that tend to minimize the chances someone will give you a referral. The *Seven-Nevers* are:

1 **Ask—do not hint!** It should be a question!

2 Avoid asking with a **Closed-Ended Question.** (As in, *"Do you know anyone...?"*)

3 Avoid the word **"Interested."** (As in, *"Who might be interested in our services?"*)

4 Avoid the word **"Benefit."**** (As in, *"Who can benefit from our product?"*)

5 Avoid the word **"Help."** (As in, *"Who we can help the way we have been able to help you?"*)

6 Avoid the words **"Use/Utilize."** (As in, *"Who could use our services?"*)

7 Avoid the actual word **"Refer"** and **"Referral."** If you ask for a "referral," or ask if the person can "refer" someone, you are asking them to help *you*. It is not about you—it is about the person the client refers.

(**I cannot explain it, but I have documented the negative consequences of using this word for over thirty years.)

My experiences with applying this concept:
(See Tech #36) ➡

Date: _____

Company: _____

Client(s) Names: _____

_____

What I learned or was reminded: _____

_____

_____

Date: _____

Company: _____

Client(s) Names: _____

_____

What I learned or was reminded: _____

_____

_____

Date: _____

Company: _____

Client(s) Names: _____

_____

What I learned or was reminded: _____

_____

_____

Real-World Selling™ Technique

As Promised

The most common complaint people have about salespeople is: "You cannot count on them." This is why in every follow-up note, email, letter, voice-message, text message, etc., you should consider using the phrase *"as promised..."* to subtly let the client know you can be trusted to do what you say you will do.

After a client reads or hears the phrase "as promised..." two or three times, they tend to naturally begin to assume you are someone who can be trusted.

For example:

a   *"As promised, here is my business card for your files."*

b   *"As promised, I have forwarded your application to John Smith in our Memphis office and he assured me he will call you this afternoon."*

c   *"As promised, I am calling to confirm our meeting."*

My experiences with applying this concept:

(See Tech #36) ➤

Date: _____

Company: _____

Client(s) Names: _____

_____

What I learned or was reminded: _____

_____

_____

Date: _____

Company: _____

Client(s) Names: _____

_____

What I learned or was reminded: _____

_____

_____

Date: _____

Company: _____

Client(s) Names: _____

_____

What I learned or was reminded: _____

_____

_____

Real-World Selling™ Technique

Involve the Referring Person

Most people prefer to tell their friend or associate when they've given someone else their name. When the referring person tells the referral to expect your call, everyone benefits.

Reasons to involve your referrer:

1 **You benefit** because the referring person may say positive things about you that you could never say about yourself. They may even do half the selling for you. Plus, as they brag about you to justify your pending call, the referring person will reinforce their own commitment to you. *(If a person recommends you to others, how can that person then do business with your competitor?)*

2 **The referring person benefits** because they keep their credibility or reputation with the person to whom you are being referred.

3 **The referral benefits** because they will appreciate the "heads-up" before you call.

My experiences with applying this concept:
(See Tech #36)

Date: _____

Company: _____

Client(s) Names: _____

_____

What I learned or was reminded: _____

_____

_____

Date: _____

Company: _____

Client(s) Names: _____

_____

What I learned or was reminded: _____

_____

_____

Date: _____

Company: _____

Client(s) Names: _____

_____

What I learned or was reminded: _____

_____

_____

Real-World Selling™ Technique

41

Keep the Referring Person in the Loop

Always keep the person who referred you informed—after all, they made a special point to tell a friend or associate that you were going to call, so it is their reputation that is at stake.

After you contact the person who was referred to you, always let the referring person know you actually lived up to their (and your) commitment.

When keeping the referring person in the loop, you should not share anything personal about the referred person, but you should at least report back that you have spoken to them.

The follow-up call to the referring person tends to be appreciated—plus, there is often an added bonus: This extra conversation often generates even more referrals!

My experiences with applying this concept:
(See Tech #36)

Date: _____

Company: _____

Client(s) Names: _____

_____

What I learned or was reminded: _____

_____

_____

Date: _____

Company: _____

Client(s) Names: _____

_____

What I learned or was reminded: _____

_____

_____

Date: _____

Company: _____

Client(s) Names: _____

_____

What I learned or was reminded: _____

_____

_____

Real-World Selling™ Technique

Confirming Appointments

General Rule: Try to avoid confirming your appointments. *(This is a controversial recommendation, so you will need to make your own decision about it.)*

The problem with confirming appointments is that it can give the client a convenient opportunity to cancel.

Confirm appointments only when:

1 You tell the client that you will confirm it; or
2 The cost of being stood up is not worth the client's possible feeling of guilt or obligation.

If you *do* choose to confirm an appointment, do so at least three or more business days prior to the appointment. The closer you are to the appointed time, the less convenient the appointment is for the client.

(This is also another good opportunity to use Tech #39: "As promised, I am calling to confirm our meeting on Thursday.")

My experiences with applying this concept:
(See Tech #36)

Date: _____

Company: _____

Client(s) Names: _____

_____

What I learned or was reminded: _____

_____

_____

Date: _____

Company: _____

Client(s) Names: _____

_____

What I learned or was reminded: _____

_____

_____

Date: _____

Company: _____

Client(s) Names: _____

_____

What I learned or was reminded: _____

_____

_____

Real-World Selling™ Technique

Negative Emotion Words

Words create images in the minds of others, so be careful not to use the words below as they tend to create *negative images* with the client—if even subconsciously:

a **Price**: This word implies that money goes out, but nothing necessarily comes back. Use the word "investment" if possible.

b **Cost**: Do not associate yourself with something the client may be trying to cut. Instead, use the words "amount" or "total."

c **Contract**: Instead, refer to it as "paperwork" or "agreement." Contracts can land you in court.

d **Sign**: The word "**sign**" tends to make people cautious. Try the words "approve" or "write your name" instead. *(Perhaps you've heard people say, "Do not sign anything until you have read it," or, "Don't sign anything until your attorney looks at it.")*

e **Deal**: This word cheapens your idea and tends to make people skeptical. "Offer" is a better choice.

My experiences with applying this concept:
(See Tech #36)

Date: _____

Company: _____

Client(s) Names: _____

_____

What I learned or was reminded: _____

_____

_____

Date: _____

Company: _____

Client(s) Names: _____

_____

What I learned or was reminded: _____

_____

_____

Date: _____

Company: _____

Client(s) Names: _____

_____

What I learned or was reminded: _____

_____

_____

Real-World Selling™ Technique

Describing the Price

You wouldn't say, *"He ran fast,"* if everyone ran the same speed, would you? Frequently, salespeople describe the price of their product or service at their own peril when using phrases such as:

a   *Our **normal** price is…*

b   *The **typical** price is…*

c   *It **usually** sells for…*

d   *The **regular** price is…*

e   *Our **standard** price is…*

By using the words above to describe your price, it tells the client there are other prices available. So, when you tell a client, *"The **list** price is X,"* don't be surprised if the client asks, *"Can we get a better price?"*

Instead, when asked about the price, simply say, *"It is X." (Simple, short, definite, and no description.)*

My experiences with applying this concept:

(See Tech #36)

Date: _____

Company: _____

Client(s) Names: _____

_____

What I learned or was reminded: _____

_____

_____

Date: _____

Company: _____

Client(s) Names: _____

_____

What I learned or was reminded: _____

_____

_____

Date: _____

Company: _____

Client(s) Names: _____

_____

What I learned or was reminded: _____

_____

_____

Real-World Selling™ Technique

Interests and Specifics

Salespeople tend to focus on only business reasons to contact their clients. But, you can also let the client know that you value them for more than just business.

To do this, add two fields to your client or contact database:

1 Interests
2 Specifics

To use these fields, for example:

a The client's interest may be "skiing."
  But the specific is "snow" or "water."

b The client's interest may be "motorcycles."
  But the specific is "dirt bikes" or "racing."

c The client's interest may be "boats."
  But the specific is "power" or "sail."

Once you know the clients' interest and specifics, read newspapers and magazines with them in mind. Send or deliver articles so they know you are thinking about them. Let the client know it is not only their money you care about—because good relationships are built on more than just business!

My experiences with applying this concept:
(See Tech #36) ➡️

Date: _____

Company: _____

Client(s) Names: _____

_____

What I learned or was reminded: _____

_____

_____

Date: _____

Company: _____

Client(s) Names: _____

_____

What I learned or was reminded: _____

_____

_____

Date: _____

Company: _____

Client(s) Names: _____

_____

What I learned or was reminded: _____

_____

_____

Real-World Selling™ Technique

Call Someone Who Did Not Buy

There are very few *absolutes* when it comes to relationships, but there is one *absolute* that everyone can always count on: All relationships go through phases.

Call someone who didn't buy from you six months ago, or even last year. Who knows…? Maybe their situation has changed.

Here is a statistic to consider:

80% of all sales are made after the fifth, "No;" but 80% of all salespeople give up after hearing the first, "No."**

Realize it does not have to be *your* fifth, "No," either. The client may have said, "No," to four of your competitors since you last spoke.

*(**This statistic reeks of the all-too-easy-to-justify "80/20 Rule." And, while I do not know if it is exactly correct, I suspect is the percentages are not too far off.)*

My experiences with applying this concept:
(See Tech #36)

Date: _____

Company: _____

Client(s) Names: _____

_____

What I learned or was reminded: _____

_____

_____

Date: _____

Company: _____

Client(s) Names: _____

_____

What I learned or was reminded: _____

_____

_____

Date: _____

Company: _____

Client(s) Names: _____

_____

What I learned or was reminded: _____

_____

_____

Real-World Selling™ Technique

Rule of Six

A person who does not ask questions about your idea is not seriously considering it. The "Rule of Six" is: A client who asks at least six business questions is more likely to buy.

Business questions are those questions for which the client needs answers to make a decision—not: *"How are you today?"* or *"Can I get you a drink?"*

*(I have observed the Rule of Six with clients for over twenty years, although I cannot explain why the magic number is **six** questions.)*

Of course, it makes sense that the more questions someone asks, the more likely they are considering your idea.

This doesn't always mean that someone who only asks five business questions will not do business with you. Nor, that someone who asks seven questions will buy. It simply means that once the client asks six business questions, the odds are much more in your favor for making a sale.

(That's weird, huh?)

Test the Rule of Six. Count the client's business questions.

My experiences with applying this concept:

(See Tech #36)

Date: _____

Company: _____

Client(s) Names: _____

_____

What I learned or was reminded: _____

_____

_____

Date: _____

Company: _____

Client(s) Names: _____

_____

What I learned or was reminded: _____

_____

_____

Date: _____

Company: _____

Client(s) Names: _____

_____

What I learned or was reminded: _____

_____

_____

Real-World Selling™ Technique

Ask to be Introduced

Most salespeople do not know enough people within their accounts. Before you leave your client's office, ask the client to introduce you to someone you do not know.

Here is a test:

Think about your largest account. How many people do you know in that account that you could approach and talk to about almost anything? *(The most common answer is five to ten.)*

Now, think about your fifth largest account. How many people in that company could you approach and talk to about almost anything? *(The most common answer is one or two.)*

Get to know more people in every account. You never know when people will get promoted or when positions will change.

My experiences with applying this concept:
(See Tech #36)

Date: _____

Company: _____

Client(s) Names: _____

_____

What I learned or was reminded: _____

_____

_____

Date: _____

Company: _____

Client(s) Names: _____

_____

What I learned or was reminded: _____

_____

_____

Date: _____

Company: _____

Client(s) Names: _____

_____

What I learned or was reminded: _____

_____

_____

Real-World Selling™ Technique

Testimonial Book

How persuasive would it be for potential clients to read 50-100 comments about how pleased other people are with your product or service?

Ask your clients to write their opinion of your product or service on the back of their business card. Put all the cards in a book and when a prospective client is hesitant, let them look through the book. The comments alone may do half (or more) of the selling for you.

The cards are more efficient than testimonial letters. They are personal (handwritten), quick to read and, often, people will scan dozens of cards. Plus, clients rarely date the card, so you can use it for years.

If you are asked what you will do with it, simply show them the book and explain how you will use it.

(No one has ever refused to write their opinion on the back of their card for me.)

My experiences with applying this concept:
(See Tech #36) ⟹

Date: _____

Company: _____

Client(s) Names: _____

_____

What I learned or was reminded: _____

_____

_____

Date: _____

Company: _____

Client(s) Names: _____

_____

What I learned or was reminded: _____

_____

_____

Date: _____

Company: _____

Client(s) Names: _____

_____

What I learned or was reminded: _____

_____

_____

Real-World Selling™ Technique

A Quick Moment

When the client answers the telephone, immediately ask, *"Do you have a quick moment to talk?"*

The client may say, *"No,"* but more often, the client will ask, *"What is this about?"* which is your opening to state the purpose of your call. (See Tech #2)

If the client doesn't have time, it is usually true since, at this point, they won't know who you are or why you're calling yet.

So, if the client says, "No," simply reply, *"I understand. When would be a better time [Insert a time] to call you back?"*

For example:

> *"When would be better time tomorrow before 11:00 a.m. to call you back?"*

When you reference a specific time or date, the typical reaction is, *"Well, what is this about?"*

My experiences with applying this concept:
(See Tech #36)

Date: _____

Company: _____

Client(s) Names: _____

_____

What I learned or was reminded: _____

_____

_____

Date: _____

Company: _____

Client(s) Names: _____

_____

What I learned or was reminded: _____

_____

_____

Date: _____

Company: _____

Client(s) Names: _____

_____

What I learned or was reminded: _____

_____

_____

Real-World Selling™ Techniqu

May I Make a Suggestion?

When you want someone to accept your advice, first ask, *"May I make a suggestion?"* (Client says, "Yes.") *"I would suggest...."* Does that make sense?

There are three specific details that make the suggestion most effective. They are:

1 **May I...?**: The question is far better than saying, "Let me," which imposes your suggestion. If the client gives you permission to make a suggestion, they will tend to feel more willing to *follow* your suggestion.

2 **Wait for the client to say, "Yes:"** If a client does not answer, "Yes," they may not feel as obligated to follow your suggestion.

3 **End your suggestion with a question**: Any question! It is easier for the client to follow your lead than to provide a lead of their own.

For Example:

"May I make a suggestion? ('Sure.') I would suggest that we go ahead and get your order entered so you can receive your materials in time for the start of your project. Can we do that?"

My experiences with applying this concept:

(See Tech #36)

Date: _____

Company: _____

Client(s) Names: _____

_____

What I learned or was reminded: _____

_____

_____

Date: _____

Company: _____

Client(s) Names: _____

_____

What I learned or was reminded: _____

_____

_____

Date: _____

Company: _____

Client(s) Names: _____

_____

What I learned or was reminded: _____

_____

_____

Real-World Selling™ Technique

Do Something

The reason most people procrastinate is because they do not want to do it badly enough.

This is also true with clients.

Salespeople frequently do not understand why the client will not make a decision. Well, the reason many clients put off making a decision is because the salesperson hasn't made them *want* it badly enough.

Procrastination easily becomes a habit that serves no one, except your competitors.

Suggestion: Pick a day of the week—any day—every week, and then make a commitment to yourself to start the day by doing something you have been putting off or do not want to do.

You will find that from there the rest of the day is all downhill!

My experiences with applying this concept:
(See Tech #36) ⟹

Date: _____

Company: _____

Client(s) Names: _____

_____

What I learned or was reminded: _____

_____

_____

Date: _____

Company: _____

Client(s) Names: _____

_____

What I learned or was reminded: _____

_____

_____

Date: _____

Company: _____

Client(s) Names: _____

_____

What I learned or was reminded: _____

_____

_____

Real-World Selling™ Technique

Odd Times

You have likely heard the comment, *"I need to go. I have an appointment about 10 o'clock."* The phrase, **"about 10 o'clock"** means within 5-10 minutes. But, it is doubtful you have heard, *"I need to go. I have an appointment **about 10:15!"***

In general, you will spend less time waiting in reception rooms if you schedule your appointments at odd times.

Avoid the hour and the half-hour; set meetings at 15 minutes after or before the hour.

Doing so gives your client the impression that you consider your time important and you will not likely waste their time. The client will also tend to greet you on time.

(Of course, there are exceptions to this rule, but for the most part, it works very well.)

My experiences with applying this concept:
(See Tech #36)

Date: _____

Company: _____

Client(s) Names: _____

_____

What I learned or was reminded: _____

_____

_____

Date: _____

Company: _____

Client(s) Names: _____

_____

What I learned or was reminded: _____

_____

_____

Date: _____

Company: _____

Client(s) Names: _____

_____

What I learned or was reminded: _____

_____

_____

Real-World Selling™ Technique

Reverse the Introduction

After introducing yourself, has anyone ever forgotten your name? Here is a way to help them remember it.

During introductions (on the telephone or in person), many people say their name and then the name of their company. For example:

> *"Hello. I am Rick Wilcoxon with Rick Alan and Associates."*

To help your contact better remember you, simply reverse the order. For example:

> *"Hello. I am with Rick Alan and Associates. My name is Rick Wilcoxon."*

(A client once told me that people would frequently ask him, "What is your name again?" But, once he reversed his name and the name of his company, they then asked, "Who are you with again, Joe?")

This simple change can help the client more easily remember your name. It also tends to add more importance to both your name and the name of your company. Plus, you will sound different than almost everyone else.

My experiences with applying this concept:
(See Tech #36)

Date: _____

Company: _____

Client(s) Names: _____

_____

What I learned or was reminded: _____

_____

_____

Date: _____

Company: _____

Client(s) Names: _____

_____

What I learned or was reminded: _____

_____

_____

Date: _____

Company: _____

Client(s) Names: _____

_____

What I learned or was reminded: _____

_____

_____

Real-World Selling™ Technique

A Copy of Your Notes

As you begin to take notes during a sales call, tell the client you will provide them with a copy before you leave. This practice has numerous benefits:

a   The client will tend to take your questions more seriously and provide more in-depth answers if they know they will get a copy.

b   You will appear more organized—and different—than your competition.

c   The client will not likely wonder what you are writing.

d   The client will have a written record of the details discussed to show their management and help justify any decisions.

e   The client can review your notes after you leave which encourages the client to relive the emotion of the point(s) of dissatisfaction once again.

(I have clients who have kept copies of my notes for years! Some industries are different though. You may want to check with your management to make sure there is not a legal reason that would prohibit you from giving your client a copy of your notes.)

My experiences with applying this concept:
(See Tech #36)

Date: _____

Company: _____

Client(s) Names: _____

_____

What I learned or was reminded: _____

_____

_____

Date: _____

Company: _____

Client(s) Names: _____

_____

What I learned or was reminded: _____

_____

_____

Date: _____

Company: _____

Client(s) Names: _____

_____

What I learned or was reminded: _____

_____

_____

Real-World Selling™ Technique

Detail Questions

Most salespeople agree that asking questions is extremely important, yet rarely take even five minutes to prepare the questions they should ask every prospective client.

Most salespeople tend to "wing it," rather than prepare their questions in advance.

(I am not referring to you, of course!)

Fifty to sixty percent of a salesperson's questions for a client should be Detail Questions, as they are one of the key types of questions needed to *qualify* the client.

Organize a list of Detail Questions—questions about the client or the client's company and industry—that you can ask every potential client.

Be prepared...do not expect success by accident!

My experiences with applying this concept:

(See Tech #36) ⟹

Date: _____

Company: _____

Client(s) Names: _____

_____

What I learned or was reminded: _____

_____

_____

Date: _____

Company: _____

Client(s) Names: _____

_____

What I learned or was reminded: _____

_____

_____

Date: _____

Company: _____

Client(s) Names: _____

_____

What I learned or was reminded: _____

_____

_____

Real-World Selling™ Technique

Situation Questions

Situation Questions should be Open-Ended and are designed to uncover or identify a client's possible point of dissatisfaction.

Prepare a list of at least fifteen Situation Questions involving different possible points of dissatisfaction.

You will not need to ask them all during every sales call, but that does not mean you should not be prepared!

Examples of Situation Questions:

a *"How do you feel about the level of service you receive?"*

b *"How often do you have to deal with backorders?"*

c *"When was the last time you did not receive the type of quality you expected?"*

d *"What was the most disruptive surprise you faced with your last project?"*

My experiences with applying this concept:

(See Tech #36)

Date: _____

Company: _____

Client(s) Names: _____

_____

What I learned or was reminded: _____

_____

_____

Date: _____

Company: _____

Client(s) Names: _____

_____

What I learned or was reminded: _____

_____

_____

Date: _____

Company: _____

Client(s) Names: _____

_____

What I learned or was reminded: _____

_____

_____

Real-World Selling™ Technique

Solution-Related Questions

Prepare a list of at least ten Solution-Related Questions.

These questions can be past or future tense and their purpose is to encourage the client to imagine a solution to their point(s) of dissatisfaction.

Examples of Solution-Related Questions:

a *"How did you get that resolved?" (Past-tense)*

b *"How can we get this resolved?" (Future-tense)*

c *"What can we do to make sure this does not happen again?" (Future-tense)*

d *"What were you hoping for?" (Past-tense)*

e *"What would be a better option?" (Future-tense)*

Solution-Related Questions should be asked sparingly as only three to five percent of your questions should be of this type. And, only ask them after thoroughly discussing the client's point(s) of dissatisfaction.

My experiences with applying this concept:
(See Tech #36)

Date: _____

Company: _____

Client(s) Names: _____

_____

What I learned or was reminded: _____

_____

_____

Date: _____

Company: _____

Client(s) Names: _____

_____

What I learned or was reminded: _____

_____

_____

Date: _____

Company: _____

Client(s) Names: _____

_____

What I learned or was reminded: _____

_____

_____

Real-World Selling™ Techniqu

Qualification Summary

After asking all of your questions, be sure to summarize what you have learned.

Avoid summarizing what the client *wants*, but rather focus on the issues that *cause* the client to want it.

Structure of the Qualification Summary:

"As I understand your situation... (Point of dissatisfaction)

Which means.... (Problem)

Is causing you (or your).... (Another problem)

And as a result.... (Ultimate problem)

Is that a fair assessment? (End with a question)"

You may wish to reword the example above to fit your personality. But, it is important to let the client know that you have been listening, that you understand their point(s) of dissatisfaction, as well as the causes and consequences involved.

My experiences with applying this concept:
(See Tech #36) ➤

Date: _____

Company: _____

Client(s) Names: _____

_____

What I learned or was reminded: _____

_____

_____

Date: _____

Company: _____

Client(s) Names: _____

_____

What I learned or was reminded: _____

_____

_____

Date: _____

Company: _____

Client(s) Names: _____

_____

What I learned or was reminded: _____

_____

_____

Real-World Selling™ Technique

Referral Letter

This Referral Letter works because it is written with humor, but the recipient understands that you are serious.

*(Send this handwritten, stamped letter prior to any insignificant holiday—avoid Christmas and your birthday, and **do not** send this via email.)*

Dear (First Name),

I realize you are probably losing sleep worrying about what to get your favorite salesperson for (St. Patrick's Day, Flag Day, Arbor Day, Veterans Day, etc.).

Let me make this easy for you.

The best gift you can give me is the names of three people who might like to know about our services (product, etc.).

Please write their names on the bottom of this letter and I will call in a few days to find out what my gift is.

Thank you in advance for your generosity.

Sincerely,

Your name
PS: Now—get some sleep!

My experiences with applying this concept:
(See Tech #36)

Date: _____

Company: _____

Client(s) Names: _____

_____

What I learned or was reminded: _____

_____

_____

Date: _____

Company: _____

Client(s) Names: _____

_____

What I learned or was reminded: _____

_____

_____

Date: _____

Company: _____

Client(s) Names: _____

_____

What I learned or was reminded: _____

_____

_____

Real-World Selling™ Technique

Buying Signals

A Buying Signal is defined as: Anything the client says or does that indicates they might be ready to buy. Buying Signals occur in different forms—verbal (spoken) and physical (action)—and can be structured as a question or statement.

Examples of Buying Signals:

Verbal

a *"Is there a minimum order?"*

b *"I was not aware of that."*

c *"I like that."*

d *"I wasn't expecting that."*

e *"What if we do this and have a problem with…?"*

Physical

f The client introduces you to an associate.

g The client glances through the brochure.

Prepare a list of 15 Buying Signals the client might convey, so if a client expresses a Buying Signal, you will be more likely to recognize it.

When recognizing a Buying Signal, you may want to test it with a Trial Close. (See Tech #62)

My experiences with applying this concept:
(See Tech #36)

Date: _____

Company: _____

Client(s) Names: _____

_____

What I learned or was reminded: _____

_____

_____

Date: _____

Company: _____

Client(s) Names: _____

_____

What I learned or was reminded: _____

_____

_____

Date: _____

Company: _____

Client(s) Names: _____

_____

What I learned or was reminded: _____

_____

_____

Real-World Selling™ Techniqu

Trial Closes

A Trial Close is designed to solicit an *opinion,* rather than a *decision* or a *commitment.* It can be used any time you do not know what the client's opinion is.

Be aware that if the Trial Close provides you any insight to the client's opinion, it worked—whether the client's opinion is positive or negative.

Examples of Trial Closes:

a *"How do you feel about this?"*

b *"Are there any changes you would like to make?"*

c *"Is there any reason you wouldn't do this?"*

d *"What do you suppose your management will say about this?"*

e *"What do you like most about it?"*

Prepare a list of 15 Buying Signals you could employ, so you will be less likely to hesitate when using one and can also better remember to use them.

My experiences with applying this concept:

(See Tech #36)

Date: _____

Company: _____

Client(s) Names: _____

_____

What I learned or was reminded: _____

_____

_____

Date: _____

Company: _____

Client(s) Names: _____

_____

What I learned or was reminded: _____

_____

_____

Date: _____

Company: _____

Client(s) Names: _____

_____

What I learned or was reminded: _____

_____

_____

Real-World Selling™ Technique

Does the Client Know that I Know...?

A client needs to know three things about *you*:

1 *You know their point(s) of dissatisfaction.* Too many salespeople try to sell their product or service before learning whether the client even has a real need for it.

2 *You know the cause(s) of their point(s) of dissatisfaction.* As soon as the client expresses a point of dissatisfaction, the typical salesperson immediately launches into "presentation mode," rather than ask further questions to learn more about the point(s) of dissatisfaction.

3 *You know the consequences of their point(s) of dissatisfaction.* Don't only learn the causes of the P.O.D.; determine how difficult the situation is for the client.

(When the client realizes that you know their point(s) of dissatisfaction, the causes and the consequences of the P.O.D., they will tend to become more trusting of your solution.)

My experiences with applying this concept:
(See Tech #36)

Date: _____

Company: _____

Client(s) Names: _____

_____

What I learned or was reminded: _____

_____

_____

Date: _____

Company: _____

Client(s) Names: _____

_____

What I learned or was reminded: _____

_____

_____

Date: _____

Company: _____

Client(s) Names: _____

_____

What I learned or was reminded: _____

_____

_____

Real-World Selling™ Technique

Leave No Doubt

People often hesitate to buy because they are uncertain how much the salesperson really *wants* their business.

One way to avoid this misunderstanding is to say to the client:

"We want your business and would appreciate the opportunity to work with you. Will you give us a chance?"

Notice at the end of that sentence is a question. Without the question, the comment is nothing more than a hint. *(Remember to end all answers with a question.* See Tech [#]1)

Of course, you would only want to say that to a client after you have recognized enough Buying Signals to be confident of their decision. (See Tech [#]61)

Make sure there is no doubt in your client's mind that you want their business.

My experiences with applying this concept:
(See Tech #36)

Date: _____

Company: _____

Client(s) Names: _____

_____

What I learned or was reminded: _____

_____

_____

Date: _____

Company: _____

Client(s) Names: _____

_____

What I learned or was reminded: _____

_____

_____

Date: _____

Company: _____

Client(s) Names: _____

_____

What I learned or was reminded: _____

_____

_____

Real-World Selling™ Technique

Stand at a Slight Angle

A difference between men and women is in how they position themselves with people they do not know well.

(This positioning will differ among cultures, so this advice refers specifically to the American culture.)

If the person you are trying to put at ease is a man, stand at a slight angle and a little more than an arm's distance away from him. (See Tech #66 for where to stand when meeting a woman).

Avoid standing directly in front of him, as that can make him feel uncomfortable, or even threatened.

If you are a woman, standing at a slight angle to the man may make you feel awkward. But remember, it is the other person that you want to put at ease.

(Of course, there are exceptions, although it is a good general rule.)

My experiences with applying this concept:
(See Tech #36)

Date: _____

Company: _____

Client(s) Names: _____

_____

What I learned or was reminded: _____

_____

_____

Date: _____

Company: _____

Client(s) Names: _____

_____

What I learned or was reminded: _____

_____

_____

Date: _____

Company: _____

Client(s) Names: _____

_____

What I learned or was reminded: _____

_____

_____

Real-World Selling™ Technique

Stand Directly in Front

Women prefer to be positioned directly in front of you, about an arm's distance away.

(This positioning will differ among cultures, so this advice refers specifically to the American culture.)

If the person you are trying to put at ease is female, square your shoulders with hers and stand directly in front of her. Also, stand about an arm's distance away. (See Tech #65 for men).

Avoid standing at an angle to the female, as it may make her uncomfortable or get the feeling you are not listening.

If you are a man, standing directly in front of the woman and only an arm's distance apart, may make you feel awkward. But remember, it is the other person that you want to put at ease.

(Of course, there are exceptions, although it is a good general rule.)

My experiences with applying this concept:
(See Tech #36)

Date: _____

Company: _____

Client(s) Names: _____

_____

What I learned or was reminded: _____

_____

_____

Date: _____

Company: _____

Client(s) Names: _____

_____

What I learned or was reminded: _____

_____

_____

Date: _____

Company: _____

Client(s) Names: _____

_____

What I learned or was reminded: _____

_____

_____

Real-World Selling™ Technique

Have a Seat

Let us suppose at your **first** client meeting a receptionist tells you to *"Have a seat; I will let him (her) know you are here."* As you turn, you see numerous places available for you to sit.

So, which seat do you choose? None!

Position yourself somewhat near—but not too close—to the receptionist. When the client enters the room, you want to be at eye-level with the client and appear to be ready.

It is all about your first impression!

(When my clients enter their reception room, they often look at me and ask, "Are you Rick?" There may be five or six other salespeople sitting in the room, but because I am standing and appear to be ready, they automatically assume that I am Rick.)

My experiences with applying this concept:

(See Tech #36)

Date: _____

Company: _____

Client(s) Names: _____

_____

What I learned or was reminded: _____

_____

_____

Date: _____

Company: _____

Client(s) Names: _____

_____

What I learned or was reminded: _____

_____

_____

Date: _____

Company: _____

Client(s) Names: _____

_____

What I learned or was reminded: _____

_____

_____

Real-World Selling™ Technique

Eye-Contact

Everyone has had the experience of meeting someone who didn't look them in the eye as they shook hands.

When you meet someone and do not give them eye-contact for two seconds—during the first two seconds—they tend to feel slighted. And, the message you are sending to them is that you are not interested.

Also, be careful to not be distracted when the client enters the room. Make eye-contact first, for at least two seconds, and when the client turns to walk away, then grab your briefcase and/or whatever else you have brought with you and follow.

Even more important than making "eye-contact" is making "pupil-contact." You should also know the color of the client's eyes after meeting them. Test yourself—see if you do!

My experiences with applying this concept:

(See Tech #36)

Date: _____

Company: _____

Client(s) Names: _____

_____

What I learned or was reminded: _____

_____

_____

Date: _____

Company: _____

Client(s) Names: _____

_____

What I learned or was reminded: _____

_____

_____

Date: _____

Company: _____

Client(s) Names: _____

_____

What I learned or was reminded: _____

_____

_____

Real-World Selling™ Technique

Entertainment Options

Basically, there are three dining options for entertaining clients:

a Breakfast   b Lunch   c Dinner

Each of the meals noted have advantages and disadvantages but, generally, breakfast is your best bet.

Here are a few reasons why:

a   Going out to breakfast is a treat. Most people rarely go out to breakfast during the work week. Taking a client to lunch is a very common business practice, and sometimes even expected.

b   You meet with the client before they get to their office, where situations arise causing the client to have to cancel.

c   It's cheaper. Two people can often eat breakfast for the same price of one lunch; or dinner, where you may even spend five to ten times as much.

d   The salesperson gets out of the house early in the day, allowing more time to meet with additional clients.

My experiences with applying this concept:

(See Tech #36)

Date: _____

Company: _____

Client(s) Names: _____

_____

What I learned or was reminded: _____

_____

_____

Date: _____

Company: _____

Client(s) Names: _____

_____

What I learned or was reminded: _____

_____

_____

Date: _____

Company: _____

Client(s) Names: _____

_____

What I learned or was reminded: _____

_____

_____

Real-World Selling™ Techniqu

The *Real* Objection

Have you ever had someone voice an objection? You answer it. They voice another objection. You answer that one too, and it goes on until you either give up or discover the real issue. Would it not make more sense to learn the *real* objection first?

Here's how:

1 **C**ushion: Respect the negative. (See Tech #31)
2 **C**larify: Encourage the client to talk about it.
3 **C**onfirm: Isolate the objection.

> 1 In **A**ddition…
> ("*In addition to this, do you have any other concerns?*")
>
> 2 **A**ssuming… (or If…)
> ("*If this could be addressed, would that make a difference?*")
> If the client says, "Yes," you are most likely hearing the *real* objection, but if the client hesitates or says, "No," then continue to Step 3.
>
> 3 **A**pparently…
> ("*Apparently, you have another concern. Will you tell me what it is that is bothering you?*")

My experiences with applying this concept:

(See Tech #36)

Date: _____

Company: _____

Client(s) Names: _____

_____

What I learned or was reminded: _____

_____

_____

Date: _____

Company: _____

Client(s) Names: _____

_____

What I learned or was reminded: _____

_____

_____

Date: _____

Company: _____

Client(s) Names: _____

_____

What I learned or was reminded: _____

_____

_____

Real-World Selling™ Technique

Prospects

If someone is doing business with you, they are called a "customer" or a "client."

If they are not doing business with you, but may have potential, they are typically referred to as a "prospect." These terms are standard jargon in the sales industry.

Here is a question for you though: Would you call someone a "prospect" to their face?

Of course you wouldn't, but why not?

Because you inherently know it is a disrespectful term—however, it's okay to call them a "prospect" behind their back, right? Wrong.

By changing the term "prospect" to "prospective client," "potential client," or even "client," in time, **you** will begin to feel more respectful of them.

(Using the new term will not have an effect on your clients—but over time it will affect your attitude toward them.)

My experiences with applying this concept:
(See Tech #36)

Date: _____

Company: _____

Client(s) Names: _____

_____

What I learned or was reminded: _____

_____

_____

Date: _____

Company: _____

Client(s) Names: _____

_____

What I learned or was reminded: _____

_____

_____

Date: _____

Company: _____

Client(s) Names: _____

_____

What I learned or was reminded: _____

_____

_____

Real-World Selling™ Technique

Practice Responding to Objections

On average, salespeople only hear about five or six different objections—but, they hear them over and over again.

What is surprising, though, is that when salespeople hear one of these objections, they're perplexed about how to respond to it!

This is not rocket surgery!

Here's a novel idea: Plan your responses for the most common objections you hear. Then practice them at least ten times per day, until you know them by heart. If they are not working well, you can make changes to them. But, if they do work to your satisfaction, write them down so you will have a record of them.

(Eventually, you will get comfortable with your responses and likely make subtle changes to them; therefore, keep the original record so that you can reference it if you begin to have less success.)

My experiences with applying this concept:

(See Tech #36)

Date: _____

Company: _____

Client(s) Names: _____

_____

What I learned or was reminded: _____

_____

_____

Date: _____

Company: _____

Client(s) Names: _____

_____

What I learned or was reminded: _____

_____

_____

Date: _____

Company: _____

Client(s) Names: _____

_____

What I learned or was reminded: _____

_____

_____

Compliments

Everyone likes to hear something nice about themselves, especially if they didn't know it or if they think you noticed.

When paying a compliment, you should always be sincere. However, sometimes a compliment can fall "flat." The person may not interpret the compliment in the way you meant, or they may even question your motives.

To avoid misunderstandings, and have the compliment more readily accepted, apply these three steps whenever you're giving a compliment:

1 **Pay the compliment.** (Don't explain it first.)

2 **Explain why** you paid the compliment. (This reinforces your sincerity.)

3 **Ask an Open-Ended Question about the compliment.** (This also reinforces your sincerity, plus gets the other person involved.)

Example:

"I'm impressed with the positive attitude of your receptionist (Step 1). I visit offices every day and I'm seldom greeted as friendly as your receptionist addressed me (Step 2). How did you find someone with such a friendly attitude? (Step 3)"

My experiences with applying this concept:
(See Tech #36)

Date: _____

Company: _____

Client(s) Names: _____

_____

What I learned or was reminded: _____

_____

_____

Date: _____

Company: _____

Client(s) Names: _____

_____

What I learned or was reminded: _____

_____

_____

Date: _____

Company: _____

Client(s) Names: _____

_____

What I learned or was reminded: _____

_____

_____

Real-World Selling™ Technique

Your Mama Taught You Right!

General Rule: Never set anything on a client's desk or table without first getting permission.

You should also never go behind the client's desk or move anything on their desk to show them something without asking for permission.

It's not your desk! Show respect for your client's belongings and always ask first before invading their personal space or touching anything that belongs to them.

My experiences with applying this concept:
(See Tech #36) ⟶

Date: _____

Company: _____

Client(s) Names: _____

_____

What I learned or was reminded: _____

_____

_____

Date: _____

Company: _____

Client(s) Names: _____

_____

What I learned or was reminded: _____

_____

_____

Date: _____

Company: _____

Client(s) Names: _____

_____

What I learned or was reminded: _____

_____

_____

Real-World Selling™ Technique

Your Mama *Really* Taught You Right!

Avoid accepting anything to drink in the reception room—but, if the client offers you something to drink in their office, take it.

Let the client give you something. If you are offered coffee and you do not drink coffee, tell the client that, and then ask if you might have a glass of water instead.

Think about it. If someone was at your home and you offered them something to drink, and they said, *"No, thank you,"* what would you say then?

"Are you sure you wouldn't like a soft drink or a glass of water?" and they again declined.

Five minutes later, you offer again, but this time they accept. How would you feel—more hospitable maybe?

Let the client feel hospitable, too.

My experiences with applying this concept:
(See Tech #36)

Date: _____

Company: _____

Client(s) Names: _____

_____

What I learned or was reminded: _____

_____

_____

Date: _____

Company: _____

Client(s) Names: _____

_____

What I learned or was reminded: _____

_____

_____

Date: _____

Company: _____

Client(s) Names: _____

_____

What I learned or was reminded: _____

_____

_____

Real-World Selling™ Technique

Your Mama Would Be Proud of You!

If you are given something to drink in the client's office, check to see if there are any coasters to place under your glass or cup.

If you do not see a coaster, take out one of your own business cards, turn it over, and then set your drink on top of your card. (See Tech #74)

The client will likely respond by saying, *"Oh, that's all right. You're not going to hurt anything,"* and, that's probably true, but that's not the point.

The point is, what message will the client get with your simple, unexpected gesture?

It shows you are respectful of their belongings! (Or, at the very least, the client will be impressed with your manners. It can't hurt!)

My experiences with applying this concept:
(See Tech #36) ➡

Date: _____

Company: _____

Client(s) Names: _____

_____

What I learned or was reminded: _____

_____

_____

Date: _____

Company: _____

Client(s) Names: _____

_____

What I learned or was reminded: _____

_____

_____

Date: _____

Company: _____

Client(s) Names: _____

_____

What I learned or was reminded: _____

_____

_____

Real-World Selling™ Technique

Hold On to Your Brochure

Often, salespeople lose control of the sales call because they hand the client a beautifully-designed brochure as soon as the meeting begins.

Most people are visual communicators—80 to 85 percent of them. Do not visually distract your client from what you are saying.

Keep a tight grip on your brochure until you need to show something to the client, and then take it back after showing it.

Give your brochure to the client at the end of your meeting. But, before you leave it with them, write their name on it, along with any notes that may be appropriate for their reference.

Most people find it difficult to throw anything away too quickly when it has their name written on it.

This also applies to any brochure or information you send to a client. If you want them to pay more attention to your material, make sure you personalize it.

My experiences with applying this concept:
(See Tech #36) ━━━▶

Date: _____

Company: _____

Client(s) Names: _____

_____

What I learned or was reminded: _____

_____

_____

Date: _____

Company: _____

Client(s) Names: _____

_____

What I learned or was reminded: _____

_____

_____

Date: _____

Company: _____

Client(s) Names: _____

_____

What I learned or was reminded: _____

_____

_____

Real-World Selling™ Technique

Six Types of Evidence

Most salespeople believe in their product or service; yet, apparently, it never occurs to them that others may not!

There are six types of evidence at your disposal to help a client accept your idea:

a **Demonstration:** Let the client do it. (The client already knows *you* can. Make sure the client is confident that *they* can do it.)

b **Exhibits:** Brochures, drawings, photos, graphs, charts, renderings, a piece of the product, etc.

c **Facts & Statistics**

d **Examples:** Stories about satisfied customers.

e **Analogies:** Compare the unknown to the known. *"Our service agreement (the unknown) is much like the carpet on your floor (the known). We have you covered from one extreme to the other."*

f **Testimonials:** Written and/or verbal. (See Tech #49)

Evidence tends to "D-E-F-E-A-T" the client's doubts. The more of these six methods you use, the more persuasive you will be.

My experiences with applying this concept:

(See Tech #36)

Date: _____

Company: _____

Client(s) Names: _____

_____

What I learned or was reminded: _____

_____

_____

Date: _____

Company: _____

Client(s) Names: _____

_____

What I learned or was reminded: _____

_____

_____

Date: _____

Company: _____

Client(s) Names: _____

_____

What I learned or was reminded: _____

_____

_____

Real-World Selling™ Technique

Seven Methods to Capture Attention

Clients may have numerous details on their mind when a salesperson calls or shows up at their office.

The use of one or more of the following techniques can help to better focus your client's attention:

a **Ask a Question**

b **Shocking Comment:** Say something "off the wall;" something the client wouldn't expect.

c **Curiosity Opener:** (See Tips #11 & #12)

d **Compliment:** (See the Tech#73)

e **Gift:** It does not have to be expensive, especially if it is unique or unusual.

f **Referral:** Mention the person's name that referred you early in the conversation.

g **Exhibit:** Pique the client's curiosity with a part of the product, or a photo, etc.

These seven methods can be used throughout the sales call to continue holding the client's attention.

My experiences with applying this concept:
(See Tech #36)

Date: _____

Company: _____

Client(s) Names: _____

_____

What I learned or was reminded: _____

_____

_____

Date: _____

Company: _____

Client(s) Names: _____

_____

What I learned or was reminded: _____

_____

_____

Date: _____

Company: _____

Client(s) Names: _____

_____

What I learned or was reminded: _____

_____

_____

Real-World Selling™ Techniqu

Work the Chair

When meeting with your clients, pay attention to how you position yourself in the chair. Most salespeople are almost always leaning forward, even if only slightly.

Learn to work the chair to send subtle messages:

Lean Forward: When you or the client are saying something important. Make the client think that what you are saying, or what you are hearing, is important and that you are paying close attention.

Lean Back: When you want to encourage the client to open up and talk more. Leaning back in your chair lets the client know they have the "stage" and you are listening.

Of course, in either instance above, keeping good eye contact with the client is very important or the message you send instead will be one of *boredom*.

My experiences with applying this concept:

(See Tech #36)

Date: _____

Company: _____

Client(s) Names: _____

_____

What I learned or was reminded: _____

_____

_____

Date: _____

Company: _____

Client(s) Names: _____

_____

What I learned or was reminded: _____

_____

_____

Date: _____

Company: _____

Client(s) Names: _____

_____

What I learned or was reminded: _____

_____

_____

Real-World Selling™ Technique

Introduce Yourself—Really?

Have a better reason for calling—perhaps one the client might actually care about.

What is it about salespeople that makes them think total strangers want them to call and "introduce" themselves? Are they really thinking about what they're saying?

There's nothing wrong with "introducing yourself" or "introducing your company;" it is just not a good enough reason to contact a potential client.

If an "introduction" is the purpose for your call, save yourself and the client a lot time and just send your photograph and a biography!

If you believe introducing yourself is so important, here is a test for you: At a shopping mall offer to introduce yourself to everyone who walks by.

If you agree that would be a ridiculous thing to do, then why would those same people want you to introduce yourself when they get to their office?

(There is an exception though: If the client is an existing customer and your responsibilities now include working with this client, then it is appropriate to call and introduce yourself.)

My experiences with applying this concept:

Date: _____

Company: _____

Client(s) Names: _____

_____

What I learned or was reminded: _____

_____

_____

Date: _____

Company: _____

Client(s) Names: _____

_____

What I learned or was reminded: _____

_____

_____

Date: _____

Company: _____

Client(s) Names: _____

_____

What I learned or was reminded: _____

_____

_____

Real-World Selling™ Techniqı

Confirmation Questions

The purpose of a Confirmation Question is to confirm something the *salesperson* has said. A Confirmation Question is most often used during the presentation phase of the sales call, although not always. It can be either an Open-Ended or Closed-Ended Question.

For example:

a   *"Does that make sense?"*

b   *"Would you agree with that?"*

c   *"What are your thoughts on that?"*

d   *"How does that sound?"*

e   *"Am I correct?"*

f   *"Right?"*

g   *"Did I say that right?"*

In reality, Confirmation Questions are Trial Closes and they tend to solicit either a Buying Signal or an objection from the client.

My experiences with applying this concept:

(See Tech #36)

Date: _____

Company: _____

Client(s) Names: _____

_____

What I learned or was reminded: _____

_____

_____

Date: _____

Company: _____

Client(s) Names: _____

_____

What I learned or was reminded: _____

_____

_____

Date: _____

Company: _____

Client(s) Names: _____

_____

What I learned or was reminded: _____

_____

_____

Real-World Selling™ Techniqu

Acknowledgement Questions

An Acknowledgement Question is similar to a Confirmation Question (see Tech #82) in that it is normally used during the presentation phase, but different in that it acknowledges something the *client* said.

Acknowledgement Questions are usually Closed-Ended.

For example:

a *"Isn't that what you were looking for?"*

b *"Didn't you say that was what you wanted?"*

c *"Is that still your main concern?"*

d *"Does that address what you wanted to do?"*

e *"Will that satisfy your manager's request?"*

As the client continues to agree, *"Yes, that's what I wanted,"* or *"Yes, that's what I said I was looking for,"* it becomes less likely the client will refuse your idea.

Acknowledgement Questions are also Trial Closes and tend to solicit either a Buying Signal or an objection from the client.

My experiences with applying this concept:
(See Tech #36)

Date: _____

Company: _____

Client(s) Names: _____

_____

What I learned or was reminded: _____

_____

_____

Date: _____

Company: _____

Client(s) Names: _____

_____

What I learned or was reminded: _____

_____

_____

Date: _____

Company: _____

Client(s) Names: _____

_____

What I learned or was reminded: _____

_____

_____

Real-World Selling™ Techniqı

The Client's Agenda

When meeting with a client, understand that they may not always have the same agenda that you have.

After stating your purpose for calling on the client (see Tech #2), you might consider asking the client:

"What would you like to accomplish during our meeting this morning (afternoon, etc.)?"

Usually, the client will accept your agenda. But you may be surprised with the client's response and find the client has an agenda that is clearly more important—and even more profitable—than your own!

My experiences with applying this concept:
(See Tech #36)

Date: _____

Company: _____

Client(s) Names: _____

_____

What I learned or was reminded: _____

_____

_____

Date: _____

Company: _____

Client(s) Names: _____

_____

What I learned or was reminded: _____

_____

_____

Date: _____

Company: _____

Client(s) Names: _____

_____

What I learned or was reminded: _____

_____

_____

Real-World Selling™ Technique

The Client's Time

An H.R. Director for a large firm once said that while interviewing an applicant for a sales position, she would make a deliberate point to look at her watch.

She then admitted she would not hire any applicant who failed to acknowledge it when she looked. She did this because she felt if the interviewee did not respond in some way that they would likely be oblivious to the time of their company's client's as well. Right or wrong, fair or not, that is what she believed.

Anytime a client looks at their watch, or a clock, be sure to acknowledge it.

Maybe ask:

"How are we doing with the time?"

(I have found that, more often than not, the client says everything is just fine but, of course, it is possible they have some place to be and need to end the meeting.)

My experiences with applying this concept:
(See Tech #36)

Date: _____

Company: _____

Client(s) Names: _____

_____

What I learned or was reminded: _____

_____

_____

Date: _____

Company: _____

Client(s) Names: _____

_____

What I learned or was reminded: _____

_____

_____

Date: _____

Company: _____

Client(s) Names: _____

_____

What I learned or was reminded: _____

_____

_____

Real-World Selling™ Technique

Silence

Sometimes silence is the best option.

The same H.R. Director as referenced in Tech #84 said that during the first ten to fifteen minutes in an interview with an applicant for a sales position, she would ask a lot of questions. Then, suddenly, she would become silent.

She explained that she had often been amazed at the amount of information the applicant would volunteer in order to fill the silence, some of which she could not legally even ask about.

Never make a client feel uncomfortable, but realize that a little silence on occasion might encourage the client to talk more.

(I have made joint-sales calls with thousands of salespeople and have noticed that silence can make people feel uncomfortable; especially salespeople. Silence can be an effective information-gathering technique though.)

My experiences with applying this concept:
(See Tech #36) ➤

Date: _____

Company: _____

Client(s) Names: _____

_____

What I learned or was reminded: _____

_____

_____

Date: _____

Company: _____

Client(s) Names: _____

_____

What I learned or was reminded: _____

_____

_____

Date: _____

Company: _____

Client(s) Names: _____

_____

What I learned or was reminded: _____

_____

_____

Real-World Selling™ Technique

Feel—Felt—Found

There is an age-old sales technique that has been taught for many decades called the Feel—Felt—Found Response.

Here is how it works:

When the client says something negative, the salesperson responds by saying, *"I understand how you **feel**. Many of our customers **felt** the same way, until they **found** how this can really benefit them."*

If you are using this technique— STOP!

The problem with this response is that it has been seriously overused and it is very likely your client has heard it before—many times.

There are other, more viable sales techniques that are still appropriate for use today, even though the technique has been around for years.

But, should you really keep saying the same thing—**word-for-word**—after so many decades of use?

My experiences with applying this concept:
(See Tech #36)

Date: _____

Company: _____

Client(s) Names: _____

_____

What I learned or was reminded: _____

_____

_____

Date: _____

Company: _____

Client(s) Names: _____

_____

What I learned or was reminded: _____

_____

_____

Date: _____

Company: _____

Client(s) Names: _____

_____

What I learned or was reminded: _____

_____

_____

Real-World Selling™ Technique

Smile—Pause—Cushion

If the client voices a negative comment or a negative question, try these three steps (in this order):

Smile—Pause—Cushion

Smile: Not a big smile or a smirk, but just a slight grin. This sends the message to the client that you are okay, still friendly, and/or not offended. The smile also keeps your own defenses from rising, as it is virtually impossible to feel genuinely defensive while genuinely smiling.

Pause: For only one to two seconds. The message the client will receive is that you are comfortable, still in control, and giving their comment consideration.

Cushion: Show respect for the client's negative comment. This tends to drop the client's defenses and also gives you time to think before you continue with your response. (See Tech #31)

These **Smile—Pause—Cushion** steps apply whether you're on the phone or meeting with the client in person.

My experiences with applying this concept:
(See Tech #36)

Date: _____

Company: _____

Client(s) Names: _____

_____

What I learned or was reminded: _____

_____

_____

Date: _____

Company: _____

Client(s) Names: _____

_____

What I learned or was reminded: _____

_____

_____

Date: _____

Company: _____

Client(s) Names: _____

_____

What I learned or was reminded: _____

_____

_____

Real-World Selling™ Technique

Be Willing to Leave

Sometimes clients hesitate to meet with salespeople because the last salesperson said it would take only thirty minutes, yet an hour and a half later the client still could not get rid of them!

If you tell a client your meeting should only take thirty minutes (or whatever amount of time), be prepared to leave at the end of that time.

If you find you need more time than you first suggested, consider saying something like:

"I promised you thirty minutes and while our time is up, there are still a few details we need to discuss. Would you prefer to continue now or schedule another time to go over it?"

If you are talking about something important to the client, they will almost always let you continue (unless they actually have a time conflict).

My experiences with applying this concept:
(See Tech #36)

Date: _____

Company: _____

Client(s) Names: _____

_____

What I learned or was reminded: _____

_____

_____

Date: _____

Company: _____

Client(s) Names: _____

_____

What I learned or was reminded: _____

_____

_____

Date: _____

Company: _____

Client(s) Names: _____

_____

What I learned or was reminded: _____

_____

_____

Real-World Selling™ Technique

How Are You Today?

A C.P.A. once said that he hated it when salespeople asked, *"How are you today?"* When asked why that was, the reply was *"I know they don't really care how I am, so why do they always ask?"*

Good question.

If you want to be perceived to be like every other salesperson, all you have to do is *sound* like every other salesperson.

"How are you today?" is an extremely common opening question that salespeople use when calling a client or prospective customer.

Example:

> *"My name is John Smith and I work for XYZ Company. How are you today?"*

This isn't really a major mistake, but it can be irritating for someone who hears that question all day long; especially if they believe you don't really care!

Almost *any* question to open your conversation might be better than, *"How are you today?"*

My experiences with applying this concept:
(See Tech #36) ➤

Date: _____

Company: _____

Client(s) Names: _____

_____

What I learned or was reminded: _____

_____

_____

Date: _____

Company: _____

Client(s) Names: _____

_____

What I learned or was reminded: _____

_____

_____

Date: _____

Company: _____

Client(s) Names: _____

_____

What I learned or was reminded: _____

_____

_____

Real-World Selling™ Technique

Problems?

Salespeople are eager to let the client know they want to solve their client's problems. So, they ask, *"Are there any problems I can take care of for you?"*

This is really not a bad question—it is just a bad *opening* question.

Used enough, do not be surprised if clients begin to cancel appointments because they assume you just want to know if they are having problems.

This lesson is often learned the hard way.

Example:

> When a salesman was announced to one of his best clients, the client told the receptionist, *"Please just let him know that I'm real busy and that I don't have any problems right now."*

It didn't take more than that for the salesman to get the hint that the approach wasn't working as intended.

Again, salespeople may mean well, but this question does not provide a good enough reason for the client to routinely meet with them. *(The client can tell the salesperson, "I have no problems," by phone.)*

My experiences with applying this concept:
(See Tech #36)

Date: _____

Company: _____

Client(s) Names: _____

_____

What I learned or was reminded: _____

_____

_____

Date: _____

Company: _____

Client(s) Names: _____

_____

What I learned or was reminded: _____

_____

_____

Date: _____

Company: _____

Client(s) Names: _____

_____

What I learned or was reminded: _____

_____

_____

Real-World Selling™ Technique

Service

Salespeople frequently claim that, *"We provide great service,"* or *"We have the best service in the industry."* But what does that really mean?

How would you respond if a client asked, *"What do you do that your competition does not?"*

The answer you provide better be specific, and not the same vague, worn out claim everyone says, such as: *"We care"* or *"We treat our customers with respect..."* blah, blah, blah.

Sure, you mean it, but when you say it, it will make you sound just like every other salesperson who claims to provide "good service."

Do not give the client the perception that you are like everyone else. Specifically define what you consider to be "good service." Write it down and give it to your customers. (For an example, see Tech #111)

My experiences with applying this concept:
(See Tech #36)

Date: _____

Company: _____

Client(s) Names: _____

_____

What I learned or was reminded: _____

_____

_____

Date: _____

Company: _____

Client(s) Names: _____

_____

What I learned or was reminded: _____

_____

_____

Date: _____

Company: _____

Client(s) Names: _____

_____

What I learned or was reminded: _____

_____

_____

Real-World Selling™ Technique

Always a Benefit

Make a promise to each of your customers that the relationship they have with you will always be of some benefit. (See Tech #2)

Example:

> *"I'll make you a promise that every time I call on you, I'll have something of benefit to talk about with you, and I'll not take a lot of your time, all right?"*

Clients almost always react positively to this promise.

Then ask: *"To make sure you receive the kind of service you prefer, how often would you like to hear from me?"*

*(Notice that "How often would you like to **meet** with me?" was not asked. The client will be more open to "hear" from you than to "meet" with you, because it's less of a commitment.)*

If the client does not provide a time, you can suggest one yourself, and ask if it's appropriate. You may be surprised by the time frame the client thinks is "good service."

My experiences with applying this concept:
(See Tech #36)

Date: _____

Company: _____

Client(s) Names: _____

_____

What I learned or was reminded: _____

_____

_____

Date: _____

Company: _____

Client(s) Names: _____

_____

What I learned or was reminded: _____

_____

_____

Date: _____

Company: _____

Client(s) Names: _____

_____

What I learned or was reminded: _____

_____

_____

Real-World Selling™ Technique

Two or More Weeks from Now

If you want more appointments, schedule them two or more weeks out because it is easier to get an appointment in two weeks than it is for this week or next week.

Example:

Suppose someone was to ask, *"Can we meet this Friday?"*

Your answer might be, *"This week won't work."*

If they then ask, *"What about next week?"*

Again, you may reply, *"No, next week isn't much better."*

In this case, it's hard to expect someone to believe that you cannot find thirty minutes in your calendar two weeks from now.

Don't make scheduling your appointments any harder than it needs to be. Unless the client needs to meet with you sooner, set your appointments two or more weeks from now.

(Some seem to have one concern with this concept: They fear that if they don't meet with the client right away, it will never happen. Trust me—two weeks from now will eventually occur. I have never seen it not happen!)

My experiences with applying this concept:
(See Tech #36)

Date: _____

Company: _____

Client(s) Names: _____

_____

What I learned or was reminded: _____

_____

_____

Date: _____

Company: _____

Client(s) Names: _____

_____

What I learned or was reminded: _____

_____

_____

Date: _____

Company: _____

Client(s) Names: _____

_____

What I learned or was reminded: _____

_____

_____

Real-World Selling™ Technique

Proprietary Information

Never share proprietary information about one client with another client.

Telling a client any information about one of their competitors—who is also one of your customers—is "credibility suicide." It only assures that neither customer will share anything of importance with you again.

It can take years to establish trust and build credibility—but only moments to completely destroy it with one slip of the tongue.

Protect your credibility and the trust of others. It is one of the most important characteristics you will earn.

My experiences with applying this concept:

(See Tech #36)

Date: _____

Company: _____

Client(s) Names: _____

_____

What I learned or was reminded: _____

_____

_____

Date: _____

Company: _____

Client(s) Names: _____

_____

What I learned or was reminded: _____

_____

_____

Date: _____

Company: _____

Client(s) Names: _____

_____

What I learned or was reminded: _____

_____

_____

Real-World Selling™ Technique

Four Price Options

When a client has the perception that your price exceeds your value, they will often say, *"No."*

When this happens, you have four possible options:

a Drop the price   c Combination of a and b
b Raise the value   d Walk away

Guess which option is usually the first choice among salespeople? Option "a."

While there is nothing inherently wrong with lowering your price, it should never be your first option.

Salespeople are not hired to lower the company's prices—they are hired to convince people about the value the company has to offer.

Before dropping your price, at least *attempt* to do what you were hired to do!

Consider this: If there were no objections to doing business with your company, there would be no reason to hire salespeople.

(It takes exactly zero selling skills to lower the price.)

My experiences with applying this concept:
(See Tech #36)

Date: _____

Company: _____

Client(s) Names: _____

_____

What I learned or was reminded: _____

_____

_____

Date: _____

Company: _____

Client(s) Names: _____

_____

What I learned or was reminded: _____

_____

_____

Date: _____

Company: _____

Client(s) Names: _____

_____

What I learned or was reminded: _____

_____

_____

Real-World Selling™ Technique

When Forced to Drop the Price

If you *have* to drop the price of your product or service, even one penny:

1 Get Something in Return

Negotiate something from the client in return like:

- Better payment terms
- A larger order
- Future, or other, business opportunities
- Referrals

2 Make it Appear Painful *(It probably is!)*

- Grimace
- Act shocked
- Pause and then ask, *"What would be your second choice?"*

(Actually, the question, "What would be your second choice?" is my favorite. I am often surprised at what the client chooses, and if they don't have a second choice, you can always offer one of your own.)

My experiences with applying this concept:
(See Tech #36)

Date: _____

Company: _____

Client(s) Names: _____

_____

What I learned or was reminded: _____

_____

_____

Date: _____

Company: _____

Client(s) Names: _____

_____

What I learned or was reminded: _____

_____

_____

Date: _____

Company: _____

Client(s) Names: _____

_____

What I learned or was reminded: _____

_____

_____

Real-World Selling™ Technique

Reduction to the Difference

One very effective technique to help justify your price is called, "Reduction to the Difference," which appeals to how people choose between two options in the first place.

Here is how it works: Suppose your price is $1,200 and your competitor's price is $1,000. Do not sell the idea of $1,200, because the client has already accepted $1,000! All you need to sell is the $200 difference. Be sure to let the client hear you say the difference four times. For example:

1 *So, we're talking about a difference of $200, right?* (1st time)
2 *So, let's see what you get for your $200.* (2nd time)
3 *For $200,* (3rd time) *you get (benefit, benefit, benefit, benefit, benefit, etc.).*
4 *Do you see why $200 is a worthwhile investment in the long run?* (4th time)

Realize people usually only consider the difference, not the total, when considering two ideas.

(Like when buying a new car, you typically do not think, "The car costs $25,450, but for $26,450 I can get the nicer wheels." Instead, you think, "For an extra $1,000, I can get the nicer wheels.")

My experiences with applying this concept:
(See Tech #36)

Date: _____

Company: _____

Client(s) Names: _____

_____

What I learned or was reminded: _____

_____

_____

Date: _____

Company: _____

Client(s) Names: _____

_____

What I learned or was reminded: _____

_____

_____

Date: _____

Company: _____

Client(s) Names: _____

_____

What I learned or was reminded: _____

_____

_____

Real-World Selling™ Technique

Reduction to the Ridiculous

Identify the difference in price between you and your competitor first. Then determine what your client believes is the total usage of the product or service. Next divide the difference into the total use.

For example: (Supposing again that your price is $1,200 and your competitor's is $1,000.)

You: *"So, we're talking about a difference of $200, right?"*

Client: *"Yes, but I don't know if we need to spend an extra $200."*

You: *"How many of your employees do you think will use this?"*

Client: *"Probably fifty to sixty."*

You: *"How long do you plan to use the product?"*

Client: *"Well, I would think for at least five years."*

You: *"So, if only fifty employees benefit from this, over a five year period, the difference amounts to only eighty cents per year, per employee. Do you feel the additional benefits are worth eighty cents per year?"*

My experiences with applying this concept:
(See Tech #36)

Date: _____

Company: _____

Client(s) Names: _____

_____

What I learned or was reminded: _____

_____

_____

Date: _____

Company: _____

Client(s) Names: _____

_____

What I learned or was reminded: _____

_____

_____

Date: _____

Company: _____

Client(s) Names: _____

_____

What I learned or was reminded: _____

_____

_____

Real-World Selling™ Technique

The Alternative

Most salespeople spend too much time trying to solve *other people's* problems.

Instead, let the client try to solve the price issue first. If your client does not know how, then you can give it a shot! (After all, you were not the one who brought it up.)

Here is a simple approach that often works well:

"I appreciate your concern. We have a problem because we are not able to address your issue(s) of... (point of dissatisfaction), for that price and still provide you the kind of (quality, service, experience, people, etc.) that you expect. How do we work this out?"

Encourage the client to suggest another alternative first. They will often suggest an idea about twenty percent of the time. And, you may be surprised by the suggestion. If they do not have an idea, mention an alternative yourself. But, let the client try to work it out first.

My experiences with applying this concept:

(See Tech #36)

Date: _____

Company: _____

Client(s) Names: _____

_____

What I learned or was reminded: _____

_____

_____

Date: _____

Company: _____

Client(s) Names: _____

_____

What I learned or was reminded: _____

_____

_____

Date: _____

Company: _____

Client(s) Names: _____

_____

What I learned or was reminded: _____

_____

_____

Real-World Selling™ Technique

The Comparison

When confronted with the price objection, this approach and Tech #100 are favorites:

1 *"If everyone's price were the same, whom would you choose?"* (Suppose for now the client chooses you.)

2 *"I know you would be pleased with that decision, as well. Why would you choose us?"* (The client will then identify the advantages they perceive you have over your competition.)

3 *"How much do you feel those advantages are worth?"*

It is important to note that if the client does not choose you in Question 1, then your price is not the issue. Even if you match your competitor's lower price, the client will still choose your competitor. If that is the case, instead, say this:

"Apparently, you have another concern. Will you please tell me what it is?"

Realize, of course, you may never learn the client's real concern, although you may find out what it is.

My experiences with applying this concept:
(See Tech #36)

Date: _____

Company: _____

Client(s) Names: _____

_____

What I learned or was reminded: _____

_____

_____

Date: _____

Company: _____

Client(s) Names: _____

_____

What I learned or was reminded: _____

_____

_____

Date: _____

Company: _____

Client(s) Names: _____

_____

What I learned or was reminded: _____

_____

_____

Real-World Selling™ Technique

Not in the Budget

This can be a difficult objection to convert, because the client is implying that the decision is beyond their control. And, it will be easy for them to stick with that excuse, unless you can make it more appealing for the client to modify their budget.

Consider what a "budget" is. A budget is simply a plan. Mind you, it is a plan for which people are held accountable, but it is only a plan, and plans can often change.

Many times a client has said, *"I don't have this in the budget, but I'll find the money somewhere to pay for this."*

Instead of saying, "Oh well," and then giving up (like too many salespeople tend to do), respond with:

> *"I understand, because if this cost more money than it would generate for you, it might be hard to justify for any budget. What if we were talking about a small (or smaller) amount that could actually generate far more money for your budget? Would that, at least be worth talking about?"*

My experiences with applying this concept:

(See Tech #36) ⟶

Date: _____

Company: _____

Client(s) Names: _____

_____

What I learned or was reminded: _____

_____

_____

Date: _____

Company: _____

Client(s) Names: _____

_____

What I learned or was reminded: _____

_____

_____

Date: _____

Company: _____

Client(s) Names: _____

_____

What I learned or was reminded: _____

_____

_____

Real-World Selling™ Technique

Proud Surprise

It seems to make sense to have the client realize there is a very good reason your product or service costs more than your competitor's.

Example:

Client: *"You're fifteen percent more than who we're buying from now."*

You: *"Actually, that doesn't surprise me. In fact, I am surprised the price difference isn't even greater. May I ask you something?"*

Client: *"Yes."*

You: *"Wouldn't you think our competitors would love to charge the same price as we do?"*

(The client will typically respond positively.)

You: *"Why do you think they can't?"*

(The answer to that question is because the market—your customers—will not let your competitors get away with it, unless your competitors can provide the same, or better, value than you provide.)

My experiences with applying this concept:
(See Tech #36)

Date: _____

Company: _____

Client(s) Names: _____

_____

What I learned or was reminded: _____

_____

_____

Date: _____

Company: _____

Client(s) Names: _____

_____

What I learned or was reminded: _____

_____

_____

Date: _____

Company: _____

Client(s) Names: _____

_____

What I learned or was reminded: _____

_____

_____

Real-World Selling™ Technique

Reverse

The Reverse is a response that redirects the client's objection back to the client and it can be used with a variety of objections.

It will not *answer* the client's concern, but it will tend to pique their curiosity to hear your answer.

An example:

> *"I realize that we're a much smaller company than your current provider. In fact, that may be the very reason you should consider us. May I explain why?"*

You need to take it from here. Explain the reason and relate your answer to how you can better address the client's point of dissatisfaction.

(Do not expect miracles with the Reverse. Still again, this tactic is better than saying, "Oh well," and walking away. Try it!)

My experiences with applying this concept:
(See Tech #36)

Date: _____

Company: _____

Client(s) Names: _____

_____

What I learned or was reminded: _____

_____

_____

Date: _____

Company: _____

Client(s) Names: _____

_____

What I learned or was reminded: _____

_____

_____

Date: _____

Company: _____

Client(s) Names: _____

_____

What I learned or was reminded: _____

_____

_____

Real-World Selling™ Technique

We're Happy with...

Most people do not usually think about how happy they are with their current provider. So when the client tells you this, what they're really saying to you is that they're *not unhappy*.

Part of the reason people say they're happy is because they assume the salesperson wants them to stop working with their current provider and switch to them.

The following response can make it easier for the client to ease into doing business with you:

"I understand. I really didn't call to disrupt the relationship you already have. Our clients tell us that we're an especially good **supplement** *(or addition) to their current service, and we don't have to be a* **substitute** *for what they're doing.* (Do not pause.)

If it were possible to.... (State a benefit to the client.)

Would it, be something at least worth talking about?"

My experiences with applying this concept:
(See Tech #36)

Date: _____

Company: _____

Client(s) Names: _____

_____

What I learned or was reminded: _____

_____

_____

Date: _____

Company: _____

Client(s) Names: _____

_____

What I learned or was reminded: _____

_____

_____

Date: _____

Company: _____

Client(s) Names: _____

_____

What I learned or was reminded: _____

_____

_____

Real-World Selling™ Technique

Call Me... (Another Time)

The response to this objection employs the advice offered in Tech #51. The objective is to show respect for the client's request, then offer a subtle suggestion to work around it.

Example:

Client: *"Call me in a couple of weeks."*

You: *"I'll be happy to* (Cushion). *May I make a suggestion?"*

Client: *"What's that?"*

You: *"I would suggest we go ahead and set a tentative time for us to meet—maybe in a couple of weeks—and, if you prefer, I'll confirm it beforehand. That way, you can have a time that best fits your schedule* (Customer Benefit). *Could we do that?* (Question)"

(This response seems to work about half of the time—which is better than giving up one hundred percent of the time.)

My experiences with applying this concept:
(See Tech #36)

Date: _____

Company: _____

Client(s) Names: _____

_____

What I learned or was reminded: _____

_____

_____

Date: _____

Company: _____

Client(s) Names: _____

_____

What I learned or was reminded: _____

_____

_____

Date: _____

Company: _____

Client(s) Names: _____

_____

What I learned or was reminded: _____

_____

_____

Real-World Selling™ Technique

Send Information

Asking a salesperson to "send information" is simply an easy way to avoid or delay telling the salesperson, "No."

Most brochures do not help a salesperson's cause, because the client will not usually read it anyway.

Instead of automatically sending information, next time try this:

"I will be happy to (Cushion). The problem is, right now, I don't know what to send to you. We have a variety of services (products, programs, plans, systems, etc.) available, and each one meets a specific and unique requirement. As a result, our brochures tend to raise more questions than they answer. (Do not pause.)

Can we get together—just briefly—to discuss a few ideas that might...? (Mention a benefit to the client.)"

*(Notice that the Cushion used above is not, "I will be happy to, **but** the problem is..." If you say the word, "but," the client may assume that you do not care about what they want and they may take offense. See Tech #34)*

My experiences with applying this concept:

(See Tech #36)

Date: _____

Company: _____

Client(s) Names: _____

_____

What I learned or was reminded: _____

_____

_____

Date: _____

Company: _____

Client(s) Names: _____

_____

What I learned or was reminded: _____

_____

_____

Date: _____

Company: _____

Client(s) Names: _____

_____

What I learned or was reminded: _____

_____

_____

Real-World Selling™ Technique

Focus Groups

Start a Focus Group: A small association of five to six non-competing members with the specific objective to generate new business leads through the qualified contacts of each member.

Criteria for a Successful Focus Group:

a Five or six members maximum.

b None of the members can compete for the same products, services, or for the client's budget.

c Each member calls on the same type of client (position/responsibilities).

d Members must trust the integrity, company, and product/service of every other member.

Conditions for membership:

a The group meets once per month.

b Business only—it is not a social club.

c All members *must* give a total of X referrals at each meeting. The referrals can be given to one person or divided among two or more people. *(The number of referrals that seem to work is two or three.)*

d No member can miss more than three consecutive meetings.

My experiences with applying this concept:
(See Tech #36)

Date: _____

Company: _____

Client(s) Names: _____

_____

What I learned or was reminded: _____

_____

_____

Date: _____

Company: _____

Client(s) Names: _____

_____

What I learned or was reminded: _____

_____

_____

Date: _____

Company: _____

Client(s) Names: _____

_____

What I learned or was reminded: _____

_____

_____

Real-World Selling™ Technique

Work Smarter, Not Harder—Really?

You have probably heard the phrase, *"Work smarter, not harder,"* but, if you are in management, **stop telling your salespeople that!**

You may mean well, but what the salesperson hears is, *"You should not work so hard."* Instead, say to them, *"Work smarter **and** harder!"*

Would you not prefer the salespeople working for you to be smarter, plus hard-working?

Working smarter *often means* working harder—especially in a down market. It is not a question of either or… it is both!

(By the way, Managers, it is not only "a numbers game!" It is also a "quality game." A high number of lousy sales calls are worse than a lesser number of quality sales calls.)

My experiences with applying this concept:
(See Tech #36)

Date: _____

Company: _____

Client(s) Names: _____

_____

What I learned or was reminded: _____

_____

_____

Date: _____

Company: _____

Client(s) Names: _____

_____

What I learned or was reminded: _____

_____

_____

Date: _____

Company: _____

Client(s) Names: _____

_____

What I learned or was reminded: _____

_____

_____

Real-World Selling™ Technique

Enthusiasm

Enthusiasm is the second most contagious attitude there is and, because of that, many inferior products or services have been sold over the superior one.

However, there is a proper time for enthusiasm.

A salesperson should not appear enthusiastic while the client expresses their problems or concerns.

Do become enthusiastic when talking about your company and your product or service. *Show* the client you are excited about it! And, you should never expect your client to be more enthusiastic about your idea than you are.

To *be* enthusiastic, simply *act* enthusiastically. (It is that simple!) Enthusiasm breeds animation, and animation breeds more enthusiasm.

(By the way, the number one most contagious attitude is negativism!)

My experiences with applying this concept:
(See Tech #36)

Date: _____

Company: _____

Client(s) Names: _____

_____

What I learned or was reminded: _____

_____

_____

Date: _____

Company: _____

Client(s) Names: _____

_____

What I learned or was reminded: _____

_____

_____

Date: _____

Company: _____

Client(s) Names: _____

_____

What I learned or was reminded: _____

_____

_____

Real-World Selling™ Technique

Service Letter

Below is an example of a Service Letter. Feel free to tailor it for your own use. (More info, see Tech #92)

MY SERVICE POLICY.

Service! It is a word that has almost become a cliché with salespeople. If you are like me, you are tired of hearing that *claim* from people who show little evidence of actual performance. Because I appreciate your business, and realize that your success is necessary to my success, I make the following promises concerning the kind of service you can expect from me. And, I will expect to be held accountable for my performance on each of these promises.

Promise #1: Each time I call on you, I will have a specific reason for calling which will benefit you.

Promise #2: I will show respect for your time when I call on the telephone.

Promise #3: I will be on time when I visit your office(s) or will call to let you know I may be late.

Promise #4: I will be prepared when I call on you in order to maximize your time.

Promise #5: I will learn about *your business* before telling you about *mine*.

Promise #6: I will hold in strict confidence any information you choose to share with me, protecting all privileged information.

(Continued on the next page)

Promise #7: I will keep the subject of our meeting focused on business so to not waste your time.

Promise #8: I will conclude our visit quickly and when promised so as to not overstay my welcome.

Promise #9: I will enter your orders promptly and accurately to reduce the possibility of unnecessary delays and complications.

Promise #10: I will personally "walk" your order through our process when special attention is needed.

Promise #11: I will keep accurate records of your business with my company in order to better address your future requirements.

Promise #12: I will check regularly with other people within my company to make certain we honor any and all promises made to you.

Promise #13: I will immediately inform you if there is any change in the status of your order.

Promise #14: I will follow up with you to make certain you actually received the "urgent" response that may have been promised.

Promise #15: I will make you aware of any new products or services that are available which may be beneficial to your business.

Promise #16: I will quote you the best possible price—the first time.

Promise #17: I will continue to learn about yours and my businesses so your questions can be answered quickly and accurately.

Promise #18: I will immediately call you back with an answer I may not have known previously.

Promise #19: I will let you know often that I appreciate your business and will work hard to keep it.

Respectfully,

(*Your name*)

TRAINING PROGRAMS AVAILABLE FROM RICK~ALAN & ASSOCIATES

THE *REAL-WORLD SELLING*™ SEMINAR

This is a customized technique-oriented training program that focuses on persuasion skills. Entry-Level, Intermediate-Level, and Advanced-Level programs (or a combination of all three) are available to match the skill level of the participants. The recommended schedule, length of time, and instruction methods vary, depending upon your objectives. The total amount of training hours may range from 8 to over 85 hours, with a typical span of 16 to 24 hours.

THE *REAL-WORLD CLIENT RELATIONS*™ SEMINAR

This is a customized technique- and motivation-oriented training program for the individual who has customer contact, but who is not necessarily charged with sales responsibilities. The program is designed for employees such as: inside sales, sales support, assistants, engineers, technicians, accounting, and managers. As with all of our programs, the recommended schedule, length of time, and methods of instruction vary, depending upon your objectives. The total amount of training hours may vary from 8 to 28 hours, with a typical range of 8 to 14 hours.

THE *REAL-WORLD PRESENTATIONS*™ SEMINAR

This is a customized technique-oriented training program for any and all employees who make group presentations. The program is designed for employees such as: executives, salespeople, engineers, technicians, and managers. Class size is usually limited to ten individuals, although more can be accommodated. The recommended schedule and length of time varies depending upon your objectives.

INTERACTIVE WORKSHOPS

Workshops vary from 1 to 8 hours in length. Topics are selected from the various techniques taught in the three previous programs. Depending upon your requirements, we can suggest a topic to specifically address the objectives of your meeting.

AUDIO CD PROGRAMS

1 **_Real-World Selling_**™ **Skills** This is a six-CD program which includes over five hours of specific, _how-to_ ideas for selling in the _Real World_. Here are just a few:
   - Twelve common mistakes made by salespeople when calling for an appointment.
   - Techniques to learn the client's _real_ answers—not just the answers that _sound_ good.
   - Four _Magic Phrases_ to encourage answers that many buyers are hesitant to share.
   - How to better uncover hidden or potential objections.

2 **The Subtleties of _Real-World Selling_**™ In this two-CD program, Rick Wilcoxon introduces numerous critical subtleties most salespeople overlook or simply do not know.

FOR INFORMATION ABOUT ANY OF THESE CD OR TRAINING PROGRAMS PLEASE CONTACT:

RICK~ALAN & ASSOCIATES
CAREER DEVELOPMENT SKILLS

1616 Fountain View Drive
Suite 210
Houston, Texas 77057
(281) 492-1265
rickalan@rickalan.com

5515961R00130

Made in the USA
San Bernardino, CA
10 November 2013